RICHARD HOGUE

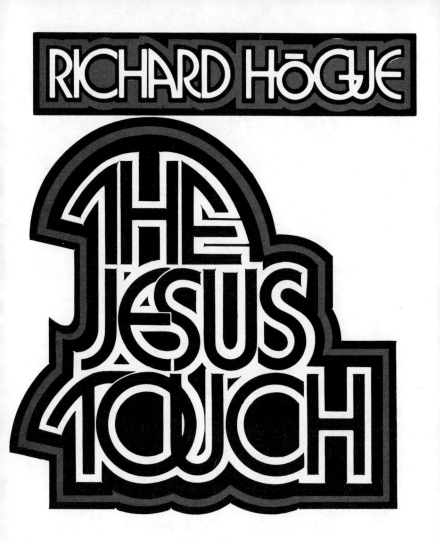

THE JESUS TOUCH

BROADMAN PRESS / NASHVILLE, TENNESSEE

*Scripture quotations are from the Revised Standard Version
unless otherwise indicated.*

Library of Congress Catalog Card Number: 72–79168
Dewey Decimal Classification: 248.5
Printed in the United States of America

Dedication

**To my fantastic Team
whose loyalty and love for
Jesus
is an unceasing source of
inspiration and joy.**

Contents

Introduction

All across America we meet a question: "How do I win people to Christ? I'd like to but I just don't know how." It deserves an answer. Not that it hasn't been answered before. It has. Authors stacked up bushels of replies, especially in the 1950's and 60's. But their conclusions constantly mislead us about how to launch effective witnessing.

Why? Because the average answer centers on a method. We hear "how to do it" in manuals, slides, pep talks. Printing presses barrage us with glad tidings of better, newer, more successful, more practical techniques. Pastors' studies and laymen's libraries overflow with mimeographed manuals describing in psychedelic terms "How to Win Souls in Three Easy Steps" and "How to Make Evangelism Calls." Sincere answers? Yes, by sincere people. But they help us like pouring more gas in the tank helps us get into a locked car.

I'm not knocking manuals, methods, and techniques. They have their place. They equip us for better work. What I'm knocking is their failure to go far enough. Try to go surfing with a snow ski . . . it may be kicks for a while, but it sure falls short of the real need. So, for two reasons, this is not a book on methods: First, we already have plenty of technique books. Second, better methods aren't the answer.

What then is the answer? It revolves around two key realities: the Holy Spirit, and the life style of the man who is controlled by the Holy Spirit. Look at it this way. Two plus two plus two equals six. And the Holy Spirit plus the personal life style, which only Jesus can give you, plus methods equals total personal witness. If you eliminate some of the two's from the two plus two plus two equation, you no longer get six. The witnessing equation adds up the same way. Why do our methods fail so successfully? They leave out two of the key factors. They do produce some (additions?), but the totals are sadly short of the possibilities.

We missed the real point when we started thinking of witnessing as an act . . . something you do. But being a great witness is much more than just an act, it is a life style. You don't say to a great football player: "Now, we don't want you to play in the first four games. Save yourself for the big game with last year's conference champions. Then we'll put you in and let you do your stuff."

No, a great football player plays all the time. If he doesn't, he either isn't one or soon ceases to be one. And we Christians have falsely separated "being" and "doing." We have disconnected "being a Christian" from "doing the Christian thing of witnessing." That isn't possible. The person who is filled and controlled by the Holy Spirit will witness as naturally as he puts on his pants in the morning . . . as naturally as a radio commentator gives the news . . . as naturally as a football player dons a helmet.

In our hectic age, we have overloaded our "doing" emphasis and shortchanged our "being" emphasis. We have tried all the latest methods. We have been busy as ticker tapes. (And when you are busy, you think you are doing great things.) But we have lost the keys. Our real need is not to organize better, call more, collect longer prospect lists. Our real need is not to learn how to do; it is to learn how to be.

The authentic question is not, "How and where do I do my witnessing thing?" The real questions are: "How do I receive that power to witness the apostles had? How does my life become so saturated with the need of men to know Jesus that witnessing becomes my complete life style?"

Everywhere this scene reproduces itself. Never has there been such a day. The world begs to know Christ. People have never been so open before . . . never had such a longing. George Harrison sings, "I really want to know you my sweet Lord." *Jesus Christ Superstar* rings out, "Who are you, what are you?" "Amazing Grace," the Christian national anthem, reaches number one on the top forty. Mass evangelism, pronounced dead five years ago, has never been so effective. Young people walk forward by the thousands.

Why is it then that our statistics act like they have the flu? Six of the nation's ten largest religious bodies report declines in membership. Even the few with slight gains (less than 1 percent) can't brag much. That is not even half as fast as the population is increasing. Since 1960, public school enrolment has been on the incline. But Sunday School attendance took a toboggan ride. Total the attendance in all the churches in your town. Then compare it to the total population. Far less than one half of the town is worshiping God each week.

The *Handbook of Denominations* in the United States reports that a small sect called the "Church of Daniel's Band" is evangelistic in character. But read on down. It was founded in 1893 and has grown to three congregations totaling one hundred and thirty-one members. And the 1970 edition of that same reference book reveals that this group no longer exists.[1] That is hardly a striking record of conversions for a church that is "evangelistic" in character. But before laughing, look at your own denomination's statistics. If current figures don't regroup, many other denominations will die a natural death shortly after A.D. 2,000.

3

A dilapidated church building in a little New Mexico town sits beside the new building. A bell once hung in the steeple house of the old unused church. But now the bell is gone. So the old bell tower just sits there, staring down on the town like an empty eye socket. How like us Christians! We have a message to proclaim to the nations . . . a message God has given us . . . one that people want to hear . . . but we aren't telling anybody about it.

We sing with gusto, "Like a mighty army Moves the church of God!" But it is a good thing we aren't a mighty army. If so, most of us would be court-martialed for insubordination. Many of us would be drummed out of the service for dereliction of duty. Perhaps it would be more appropriate to sing, "Like a mighty snail."

Why is this? In a world soaked with opportunities, why are we failing to reach people? Is it because we do not know this is our job? It can't be that. Preachers constantly tell us this is our number one duty . . . to win others to Jesus. The Bible tells us the same, "Go therefore and make disciples of all nations . . ." (Matt. 28:19) Why aren't we doing it then?

A cartoon showed a ship broken and sinking on the rocks a short distance from a lighthouse. There is no light in the lighthouse. The caption reads, "The bugs were so bad we had to turn off the lights." We do hear lots of excuses for our failure to "rescue the perishing." "But we have to work on our education department this year." "But we just don't have time!" "But our people just don't like to make calls!" "But it won't do any good!" One large church in Oklahoma told me one time when we were trying to schedule a crusade: "But that is our week for the annual budget emphasis. We couldn't have an outreach that week." Most preachers can supply you with a list of bug stories that would choke an Indian elephant.

But even though we make excuses, 99 percent of us know what our job is. We know the purpose of a church as clearly as we know the purpose of a lighthouse. We know that people unwilling to win others to Christ are like some people on welfare who can but won't work. We know that soldiers who draw their rations but won't go to war aren't real soldiers. We know that Jesus meant it when he said, "you shall be my witnesses" (Acts 1:8). We know what our job is.

Nor do we fail because we are not well-organized. We have been studied, scrutinized, analyzed, systematized, instructed, educated, directed, redirected, drilled, led, driven, pushed, pulled, encouraged. We know how to do a religious census, a telephone survey, a neighborhood canvass, evangelism campaigns, and membership drives. We are the best trained set of troops in the history of Christendom. Then why are we not winning our battles?

"Lift up your eyes, . . . the fields are already white for harvest," Jesus said (John 4:35). Nowhere, at any time, was that ever more true than today. But where are the harvesters? And why do those who go out come home with such poor yields? An accurate symbol of our "mighty army" would be a flag with big blue zeros on a white field. Why is that?

There is an answer. For years we've been relying on methods, procedures, and organization rather than a life style sold out to Jesus and saturated with the Holy Spirit.

NOTES

1. Frank S. Mead, *Handbook of Denominations in the United States* (New York: Abingdon, 1951), p. 87.

Chapter 1
"Methods: Hit or Myth?"

Running out of an office in Oklahoma City, I was already late for a golf game. Witnessing was the least thing on my mind. While I unlocked my car, a young black man walked past. As soon as I saw him, I felt God saying to me, "Witness to that guy, Richard."

Instantly, ten thousand excuses popped into my mind: Share Jesus with that guy? I'm already late. This appointment has been set for two weeks. Besides, he is a total stranger. He will probably think I'm a nut. Let his preacher win him.

So, I got into the car and drove down to the corner. The light beamed red, and traffic was heavy. Then out of the corner of my eye, there he was again. Right beside the car. When the light greened, I crept another block down the street. Another red light. I looked over. Sure enough, he had caught up. So I looked the other way and said, "OK, Lord, if he is still there after I go around the block again, I'll do it."

In Oklahoma City, it sometimes takes ten minutes to go around the block at rush hour. But when I got around the block, there he stood. So I parked the car and walked over. He was waiting for a bus. All this time I was thinking, This guy is going to think I am a nut. And maybe I am. Richard, you're out of your mind.

So, about as confident as a Model T in the Indy Five Hundred, I started in, "I know you are going to think I'm crazy, but have you ever invited Jesus into your life?"

His eyes lit up. For a split second, I wasn't sure what that meant. A man's eyes light up before he belts you too. Then he said: "No, but I have been thinking about it lately. Two nights ago, I heard this radio preacher talking about Jesus. He said I needed to . . . 'get saved' he called it. But I couldn't understand exactly what he meant by that."

As I took out my New Testament, I made a mental note to lecture myself later for lack of faith. Very simply, I shared with him what it means to be a Christian. In less than five minutes, we were bowing our heads. So, at the corner of Harvey and Robert S. Kerr in Oklahoma City, a black man named Ralph became God's man.

Finally, I got to the golf course. Bill Landers, a friend of mine, and two other men were waiting. On the fifth hole, Landers topped the tee shot, and it dropped into the creek in front of the green box. Several small kids were playing in a park beside the course. As soon as the ball hit the water, one kid offered to pull the ball out of the water for thirty-five cents. Bill said, "All I have in my pocket is a dime." Eight kids jumped in to see who could get it first.

Walking on up the fairway where my tee shot had landed, I turned to wait for Bill to make a second shot. But then I saw that Bill had all those kids around him. Instantly, because I knew Bill, I knew he was sharing Jesus with them. I started to go help him but decided that would be interfering. Anyway, I knew he could handle it.

So I turned and made my second shot . . . off to the right of the green. While I was looking for the ball, three high school kids came up over the hill. They were selling used golf balls. "Hey, man, you want to buy a golf ball?" one questioned.

"No," I replied, "but I would like to tell you about something." They changed directions and came over. We started talking about what it means to be saved. One was a Christian already. Two others had been thinking strongly about it. I led one to receive Jesus as Lord and Savior.

By the time I finished, Landers had caught up with me. Under his breath he was saying, "Praise God!" Two of the twelve-year-olds he had talked with had accepted Christ. As we approached the green, we exchanged our amazement. In less than one hour, four young men had found Christ.

Chapter 2
"No Game For Pros"

In our staff meeting a few weeks ago, we were laying strategy. God had given us a fantastic plan . . . the goal of reaching one million people for Christ in five years. It has never been done. Yet, that will only be 1/3,000th of the world's population. At that rate, it will take fifteen thousand years to reach the people alive today. Surely there is a faster way.

There is. Paul tells Timothy: "The things I have told you about Jesus, you go tell somebody else who will tell somebody else, and so on" (paraphrase, 2 Tim. 2:2). One wins one. That's God's master plan.

And it will work. If one person would go out today and win one single person, and the two go out and win one each, that is four. Then if those four win one each, that is eight. If the eight go out, that would be sixteen, and on and on. In thirty-three days, the *entire world* could be won to Christ.

The question is, Why don't we do it? The answer? Because we are leaving it to the pros. And this is no game for pros. They can't get the job done.

Look at every great religious renewal in history. None succeeded because of the pros. They happened because ordinary people, led by the Holy Spirit, won others. From Peter and Paul to John Wesley in England, every great witnessing generation has been the same. Each one went out and won another.

There are two kinds of people in the army: officers and enlisted men. A very clear distinction is made between these two kinds of persons. Unfortunately, many have carried this military attitude home to their churches.

The minister is seen as a "professional Christian" (a career officer). The layman, then, sees himself as a private who takes orders and tidies up the mess hall. He may also do occasional religious calisthenics whenever the second lieutenant thinks it advisable.

But Jesus did not define any ranks among witnesses. Jesus does not say in the Great Commission (Matt. 28), "Now some of you ought to go to seminary (which in our thinking is sort of an O.C.S. for Christians) and learn how to win people." He doesn't say, "Some of you go, and part of you stay here and pitch the tents." No, when he says, "go," he obviously refers to all hands.

All early Christians were missionaries. Not one of them, some of them, or a particular committee, but all of them. And they didn't just sit in the barracks and talk a big fight; they fought one. In only twenty years, this small band conquered a large part of the world.

How? Not because they were gifted preachers. Read some of the sermons of Paul and Peter in Acts. You won't find them especially eloquent. No, it was individuals who caught the message and took it everywhere to other individuals.

12

But what do we do today? In a certain large city church, the Great Commission is printed in the bulletin every Sunday. The congregation repeats it together at the close of the service. But witnessing in that church is almost nil; their Christian witness is limited to those who see their advertisement in the Sunday paper. And if you ask some of the members why this is, they will say: "I don't know how to do that sort of thing. I better leave that to the preacher. He is a professional." No wonder ten years of past statistics indicate that the congregation is quietly creeping into its grave.

I do not suggest that we get rid of our professional clergymen. That would be totally unbiblical. Church buildings and hymnals and Sunday Schools are not specifically mentioned in the New Testament, but we need them. And we need professional preachers too (besides, I don't want to be unemployed). But we do need to change our thinking about the responsibilities of the laymen.

I mentioned earlier the word of a song, "Like a mighty army Moves the church of God." It is a good song but a pretty bad analogy. If the church is like an army, it is the most unusual force that ever marched. In this army, there is no such thing as a leader with special privileges. In this army, every single soldier is a commissioned officer of equal rank.

All Christians are called to be witnesses and to minister. The Bible is clear on that. The preacher is a specialist in this ministry. Look at it this way: A doctor may decide to enter pediatrics, or bone surgery, or psychiatry. If so, we say he was "specialized." And a preacher is a Christian who has been called to specialize. But just as in the medical field, the average Christian still has the biggest job of ministry. He is the general practitioner. He is on the front lines. He does most of the real reaching out into society.

It was in the middle ages that people got the idea that there are two qualities of Christians. The number one quality was the professional preacher, the pastor, the priest. He and he alone, could preach the gospel. He and he alone, could administer the sacraments. Only he could conduct worship services. He was the professional. No one else could touch his holy work.

And we are getting dangerously close to that thinking again. Many laymen see themselves as some sort of assistant pastor. Their job is to keep the machine greased so the preacher can do his job (which is really their job)! If Martin Luther were alive, he would probably object as strenuously as he did in 1521.

A mother and her little girl were in the pastor's study just before Wednesday choir practice. As they talked, the organ began to play. The choir began their practice of the first hymn. The little girl, sensing it was time to go, pulled on her mother's hand and said, "Come on Mama, the church is on!"

Too many of us think of the church exactly like that . . . like a machine whose button is pushed on Sunday morning. But their church is "on" all the time, even when the people are not in the building. It is on as a Christian sits beside a non-Christian at school, works next to a non-Christian in a factory, in an office, at an oil well, or anywhere.

When Jesus healed the demoniac, he didn't tell him to become a professional evangelist. He sent him home to witness to his friends. And it brought results. (See Mark 5:19–21.) And that is where most witnessing results still come from . . . not from the pros; from average excited Christians.

We need reminding of the early Methodists when they were in their growing years. There was a time when the English aristocracy would not employ a Methodist cook. If they did, she would seek to convert the housemaid, the kitchenmaid, the parlormaid, the inbetweenmaid, and the butler. When employers begin to have that problem again today, we will soon be back to the growth rate of those years.

The Communists can teach us something here. A student is planted by the Communist party in a university. He is handed the names of twenty other students and pledged to win them to communism. If he does not do it, the party wants to know why. And he wants to know why himself.

His sense of failure will be too oppressive to live with. Does that give us a tip of why communism is growing while Christianity has been losing ground? They don't leave it to the pros. We do. And the pros can't win at this game.

A little boy visiting a large church noticed that the visitors were given a red ribbon. Each ribbon had "Visitor" on it. Afterward, the little boy asked his father, "Why don't the members get a ribbon too?" His father asked: "What would you put on the ribbons that you gave the members? You couldn't put 'Visitor' on them."

The boy's innocent reply was, "Personnel."

Not a bad idea. We are God's personnel. And there will be little forward movement of our mighty army until we start acting like it. Right now we are acting like spectators at a football game.

The door for our witnessing is not the church door. It is the door of our daily work, our daily school, our chance meetings with people. How long has it been since you stepped through that door? Some can number that answer in months; some must count it in years.

God never intended that everyone would be a preacher. For in his master strategy, the real outreach must come from the lives of Christians as they are in the world every day . . . not simply from the pulpit. Think of the outreach that even the smallest church could have if *all* of its members became missionaries simply to the neighborhood in which they live. It would mean thousands of converts every year for every church. It would mean victory after victory for our Lord, because that is where the game is won or lost . . . in the world, not in the church buildings.

A man was sitting at a restaurant counter back in World War II. Sugar rationing was in full force. "Say, may I have a little more sugar for my coffee?" he said to a waitress.

Her curt reply was, "You'll have to stir up what you have."

That is the secret to witnessing. Getting more professionals is not the answer. We must stir up what we already possess. How? By letting Jesus really have control of our total life. He will stir us up and mobilize us.

Paul wrote the Corinthians that we are "servants of Christ and stewards of the mysteries of God" (1 Cor. 4:1). That's us . . . all of us. And our solution is not to recruit *more* servants and get more *stewards*. It is in making *trustworthy* stewards out of those we already have . . . men and women who will lease their lives to the Holy Spirit.

We have been brainwashed with the lie that *individuals* can't do anything. Listen to a conversation or two and you will hear this attitude: "I know that is a problem, but what difference can one person make? What can I do about it?"

Part of the reason for our believing this big lie is our organized society. A complex culture has bred impotence in our responsibility level. But another reason is that we, as individuals, do not always wish to do anything. Some people insist on feeling like

16

"just another number." They wish to assume no personal responsibility for something God wants done. Their feeling of individual ineffectiveness doesn't come from frustration and powerlessness . . . it comes from laziness.

Shut off your negative attitude about your personal potential. You insult the Spirit of God when you pretend you are useless. The Holy Spirit plus your life style will produce a dynamic witness . . . not because of what you can do . . . because of what God can do through you.

When I was preaching our first major crusade in Houston, there were over four thousand people saved. How? It was individual people night by night who brought other individual people to Jesus. One young lady, a black girl from one of the local high schools, came in the first Tuesday night and was saved. Instantly, she started bringing her friends to Jesus. Hers was one of the only schools in which we did not have a SPIRENO Committee to bring kids to the crusade. And yet, she alone was responsible for ninety-four of her classmates finding Jesus as Lord and Savior! God didn't call a committee, he called one black girl! And she blew her school wide open with Jesus.

Remember Jesus and his little group? He did not have a Ph.D. in it. He did not have biblical scholars in it. How did Jesus manage? Because he demanded that his disciples not depend on their own ability and power . . . but instead rely totally on the Holy Spirit to be their sufficiency.

Jesus did not interview a prospective disciple by saying: "Do you have a degree from Yale? Do you have a Master's from Harvard? Did you graduate from seminary? What do you know about religion?" No, Christ just said "Follow Me! I will *make you become* fishers of men" (Mark 1:17). He didn't say, "You are pretty good at witnessing. Come and help

17

me; I need you on my staff." No, he said, "I will *make you become* . . ." In other words, "If you let me, I will take your potential and blow it into something big."

So if you say to yourself, "I am not talented," that is beside the point. Jesus doesn't mention talent as a prerequisite for a witness. If you say, "But I'm not strikingly handsome or fantastically good looking," that is immaterial. Jesus didn't mention that either. If you say, "I'm not a good speaker," you are talking nonsense. Jesus didn't ask Peter about that either. When Jesus talked to his "fishers of men," he said, "Get completely surrendered to my cause." And you can do that.

One day a small boy brought five loaves and two fish to Jesus (John 6:9). Now these fish may not have been the freshest in the world. The bread might not have won any prize at the Jerusalem County Fair. But the one powerful thing about them was this: They now belonged to Jesus, and he used them. How about your life? Are you letting Jesus use it? Or are you leaving it to the pros?

A friend of mine got acquainted with the stockroom man in a religious book store. His job was to carry heavy boxes to the cars of pastors and church members. My friend witnessed to him one day. He discovered to his surprise that the man had never had a personal experience with Jesus.

He had worked at this religious book store for months. He had come into close contact with the other employees (all church members). He worked side by side with church leaders, pastors, and denominational workers. (The store was next door to the state denominational headquarters.) But *no one* had ever asked him about his relationship with Christ! When someone did, he was ready to listen, and made a firm decision to give his life to Christ.

Why did this happen? Because my friend didn't leave it to the pros. And don't you!

Chapter 3

"Plug Yourself In"

A young man came up on the second day of a crusade. "I tried to win a friend of mine to Christ last night," he said, with a dejected look. "But he just wouldn't listen. Then I talked with another kid this afternoon. I guess it must just be me, but I can't do it."

On Wednesday evening that same boy came down front to give his life to Christ. On Thursday, he again came up to me after the service. "Wow!" he said. "I see what you mean about Jesus. Remember how I was telling you about being such a failure on Monday?" "Well, not now," he said, "I talked with the same two people today, and they both came tonight. And they got saved too!"

We see this event repeated week after week. The witness so often tries to give away something he does not have himself. Quite frankly, this is why many church members shrug the responsibility of witnessing off on the pros because they have nothing to give away. They've never been saved! You see, a Christian imitates an electrical extension cord. He passes the power of Christ to a lamp that is far away (cut off) from the wall socket. The cord generates no current alone. It only acts as a conductor, a channel, a circuit, a tool. A fancy cord is nice. Platinum plate it. Diamond stud it. But without plugging it into the wall socket, you get zero results with that table lamp.

Jesus said, "apart from me you can do nothing" (John 15:5). You are not the source of the power. You are the circuit. So if you want to witness, first plug yourself in.

The problem is that for years we've tried to make salvation so easy that we've made it easier than it really is. We've heard phrases like: "It's so easy, all you have to do is believe." "Only believe, only believe." But we have forgotten to tell people what is involved in that belief. It is not simply accepting a few facts about a man who lived two thousand years ago . . . it is not even believing that Jesus is the Son of God. The Scripture says the devils believe and tremble . . . but they're not SAVED! You see, that word *believe* is a word of action . . . it's not merely mental acceptance . . . it's a commitment. That is why the Bible says, *"Believe* in your *heart,"* not in your head. It is a commitment of the total man from your innermost being . . . a commitment of your life. It means that at the moment of salvation you must be willing for Jesus to genuinely come into your life as the Lord and Savior of your life. That's what Jesus meant when he told the rich young ruler he would have to "sell out" to be a part of the Kingdom. That is why he told Peter, "Throw down your nets and follow me." That's what he meant when he said, "You MUST be born again." Not just part of you or some of your life but you . . . every inch of you must be born again. That's what the word repentance means . . . turning from a direction going away from God and turning your life over to his direction. That's why Jesus described the kingdom of Heaven as something so valuable that a person would sell all he had to get it. Consistently, Jesus was demanding (and still does today) a complete acceptance of him as Lord (and that means BOSS) if we are to know him at all.

One reason so many people have joined the church but have not genuinely been saved is the poor counseling when people have come forward. I remember one crusade we had early in our ministry before we were using our own counseling procedure. As people would make decisions night by night, the pastor would simply sit them down, fill out a card, and then introduce them to the people without ever making sure they understood the real meaning of salvation. And the tragedy is that this has happened time after time all around the world and probably in almost every church. Then we wonder why people don't witness . . . and why so many Christians are fruitless.

Two years ago, I was in my office one afternoon when an old high school friend walked in the door. He had become a Methodist pastor. He had brought with him three of his friends . . . one an Episcopal priest, one a Lutheran minister, and another, a young Catholic priest. As they sat down and we started talking, I could not believe their story. For here were four men . . . all had been to the denominational colleges, each one of them had gone through their seminary training, they were actively involved pastoring their congregations, and yet only recently had they started to witness. The Catholic told me that for years people would come into confession and ask him what they should do for the forgiveness of their sin and he would say (in the midst of his boredom as he explained it), "Say a couple of

'Our Father's' or 'Hail Mary's' and try not to do it any more.'' But now he said, things were completely different. And the reason? Just a few weeks before our meeting, all four of these men had been saved. Think of it. Here were four clergymen who had studied the Scripture, prayed the prayers, sung the songs, but had never really met Jesus and accepted him as Lord and Savior. No wonder they couldn't witness. They had never genuinely been saved.

Make sure that you yourself have really been saved by turning your life over to Jesus and receiving him as Lord and Savior of your life. Just joining the church and being baptized . . . going through catechism . . . instruction . . . being christened . . . trying to be the best person you can . . . none of these things will make you a Christian. *Only* when you really turn your life over to Jesus, does he become your personal Lord and Savior.

All real witnessing is telling something that happened inside of you. It is not witnessing to something that happened to your pastor, or to the apostle Paul, but to you. Remove the personal and you remove the power. Has something happened inside you? Does that clue you to why you are not a high-voltage witness?

When you learn the multiplication tables, you don't rush around telling everyone about it. But if your rich uncle buys you a new Corvette, do you keep quiet about it? Hardly! You rush around to show it off. You tell people about it. The sports car, unlike the multiplication tables, landed on you personally. Church membership is great. It is good. It is helpful. You will want to do it. I recommend it. But it doesn't necessarily plug you in to the power. It doesn't hit you like a sports car. Jesus does. When he lands in your life, you will be out telling someone about it.

Leslie Weatherhead says that if a man has been

a Christian for twenty years but has never lifted pen, voice, or finger to bring another man to Christ, he is phony. He is like a man walking around on a disease-ridden island, keeping what he *says* is the cure in his pocket. There are only three explanations for such an action: Either the man doesn't believe in the cure himself; he has never tried it; or he hasn't got the real thing.[1]

When Jesus healed a deaf man, he said, "Don't tell anyone about it. Keep it quiet" [paraphrase]. But he did tell. Mark says, " . . . the more he charged them, the more zealously they proclaimed it" (Mark 7:36). Everyone Jesus healed always dashed out to tell other people. Paul, the Pharisee; Peter, the fisherman; Mary Magdalene: they all did the same. That is why the early church grew like *Jesus Christ Superstar* record sales. All the converts turned into instant mini-teletypes.

Look back to Jeremiah's time for an instant replay of today. Jews were pretty proud of their religion in 621 B.C. They had built a beautiful Temple. They had a priesthood to conduct public worship services at the Temple. They observed the proper sacrificial rituals at the proper times. They had religious holidays similar to our Easter, Thanksgiving, and Christmas. Overall, they were an extremely religious bunch.

But Jeremiah looked around and noticed that the rituals didn't generate much religion. He saw crooked business deals. He saw people running around with their friends' wives. He saw false testimony in court. He saw a degenerating society in a very religious setting. So he spoke up, "How can you stand before God in his house, and go on doing all these abominations?" (paraphrase, Jeremiah 7:9–10).

They had substituted an outward ceremony for an inward experience. That's why their culture was

24

falling apart. Have we done that too? No, we don't have a temple. But we do have church buildings. And for many people, the Christian life is the church and its "religious activities" rather than a Jesus-filled life that permeates every area of their walk out into the world.

Of course not all our church members are lost. But there is another reason why we have lost our life . . . our power. Many of our genuine Christians . . . people who have honestly surrendered their lives to Christ at some time and been plugged in . . . have shorted out!

Did you ever pick up a vacant locust skin? What a perfect mold the departing insect leaves as he sheds his former home. Looks exactly like the real thing. But there is no life in it! Many are discouraged because the church has lost popularity in the last ten years. "Our statistics are down! How terrible!" But that does not worry me. The Christian faith was born in an unpopular situation. Remember the cross? That is extreme unpopularity! Christianity grew up in disunity and turmoil. It came to maturity under persecution in the time of Emperor Nero, the later Demitian. Unpopularity has never hurt the church. It cannot now. But there is something that can hurt it . . . when its leaders and chief advocates promote and retain its original form, but lose its spirit . . . keep the shell, but lose the life and power . . . the Holy Spirit. They remind me of the disciples before Pentecost.

Notice this . . . the disciples never had power until after the experience of Pentecost. If it would have been left to them, the church would never have started. They followed Jesus. They heard him teach. But they never shared the gospel until after that day that they encountered the Holy Spirit. Remember the well of Sychar . . . Jesus and the disciples were hungry . . . Jesus waited while the disciples went into town to get the food. Think about this. Just a few miles outside of town sits the Son of God . . . the promised Messiah . . . the Creator of the world . . . the King of kings . . . and the disciples spend all afternoon in town and never tell anybody about him. (How many times do we leave him sitting in the car while we go into the grocery store . . . or leave him in the church as we face the world.) Remember when the children were crawling all over Jesus that day. The disciples were angered! They were not concerned about those children being saved. And Jesus had to rebuke them to get them to really understand.

Look at the great change! After Pentecost, they never would quit telling people about Jesus. They were thrown into jail, beaten, killed. Yet the church grew and thousands and thousands of people were saved because of their witness. What happened?

You remember when Jesus gave the disciples his Great Commission. He told them to go into all the world and preach the gospel to every creature. Now think of the impossibility of that task! Here he was telling a small group of men to do something which was totally beyond them. Go into all the world. Why it was impossible! They hadn't the money, nor the talent, nor the communications system. They didn't know the languages of the whole world. And besides all that, there was no way to get to all the world.

But there was one last command that he gave them. He told them to go and tarry at Jerusalem . . . and not to leave until they had been filled with the Holy Ghost. So really, the apostles had no choice. They couldn't go into all the world. So they went to Jerusalem to tarry and wait. And there through days of prayer, they sought God's direction and leadership and they prayed to receive the Holy Ghost which God had promised. The Scripture says that when that day came, it was unbelievable! Since they could not go into all the world, God brought the whole world to them. The Bible says they were filled with the Holy Ghost and since they didn't know the languages of all the people there that day, God just transformed their tongues and made them to speak in languages they had never heard. And because of this, there were over three thousand people saved "out of every nation under heaven."

Now many times, in thinking of what happened that day, we put the emphasis on the wrong miracle. We put the emphasis on the mighty rushing wind, or upon the cloven tongues of fire, or upon the unknown languages. But the real miracle of Pentecost was the power! And that's the promise Jesus had made. For he said in Acts 1:8, "You shall receive power after the Holy Ghost shall come upon you, and you shall be witnesses" (paraphrase). That's the miracle!

And it was that power which they received that changed their whole lives. It was the Holy Spirit.

Wonder why you don't have that power? Wonder why the church isn't winning thousands daily? Wonder why the church seems so unable to compete with the things of this world? It's because so many of us have not tarried at Jerusalem and been filled with the Holy Spirit.

But you say, "Preacher, aren't we filled with the Holy Spirit when we're saved?" Not necessarily. At salvation we are born of the Spirit, sealed in the Spirit, and indwelt with the Spirit. And all the power of the Spirit is available to every Christian. But too many believers are like a lamp that is plugged into the wall and in excellent working order . . . but the switch has never been turned on. The source is there. The power is there. But they've never let it flow.

Don't expect a preacher to recharge a church. He

won't. He can't. No one *man or method* can bring that change. The church comes alive when individual Christians make the Spirit of Christ operational in their own life style. Not before. "Not by might, nor by power, but by my Spirit, says the Lord" (Zech. 4:6). And that means, "Not by new preachers, not by new orders of worship, nor by new ecclesiastical organizations, nor by shorter board meetings, nor by more efficient systems, but by *individual people* who warm their faith at the fire of Jesus and come out new men."

Some have confused us by saying: "Our message is not relevant any more. In this modern, sophisticated, scientific age, people are just not going to buy this Jesus stuff. It's outdated. It's old-hat." That sounded reasonable until recently. But now we know it is a phony excuse for inaction. The world is crying out more than ever for Jesus. Especially among the best educated, most sophisticated young people the world has ever produced do we find this need. What is the problem? Not in the message, but in the messengers. Either they've never actually been saved . . . or they're not letting Jesus really have control day by day. Either they've never been plugged in or they've blown a fuse by not letting the real power, Jesus, through the Holy Spirit run through their life circuit.

So many Christians we talk to are as blind to the truth of the Holy Spirit as the lost are to the truth of salvation. They agree with all the terms and know all the doctrines until you really bring it down to the specifics.

One night my wife and I were sharing this wonderful truth of the Holy Spirit to a group of adults in a very wealthy suburban church. We were telling them how Christ demands that we search the very depths of our innermost being for those hidden cells of unconfessed sin and those long forgotten areas of self-control allowing God to bring to the surface for his inspection and direction . . . even the minutest areas of our life. I shared how they must be willing to really throw down their finances, their homes, their families, their jobs, their social lives, their futures . . . everything! One man said, "Preacher, you sound as though I should trust Jesus to pay my bills." I said, "You are exactly right." That doesn't mean we can be careless and foolish in such areas as finance, but it does mean that he must be our source upon which we completely depend. It means that instead of fretting and manipulating, we genuinely trust him to lead us daily . . . in jobs and profits and every other decision. You see, he demands to be KING! Not your buddy or just your pal but your KING! King Jesus reigning as sovereign in every kingdom of your life. Are you really willing to trust him in the smallest and largest areas? What about when everything is down, the skies are dark, and there looks like there is no hope? Or when everything is great and there is money in the bank, are you willing to trust him? King Jesus . . . he's the source.

One day last winter, I went out early in the morning and got into my car. It wouldn't start. I checked the gas gauge. It was full. But it still wouldn't start. What was the problem? One thing was missing . . . a spark . . . a very thin spark. Or you might call it a continuing series of sparks. And I didn't go any place until I got that spark. That's what a man who desires to witness must have . . . that tiny spark . . . that fire at the core of his life that unlocks his energy. No substitute will do. No method will replace it. No program will compensate for its absence.

A friend found Leonardo da Vinci working one morning on the unfinished painting of the Last Supper. The friend was entranced by the two silver cups on the table in front of Jesus. He remarked at the artistic skill exhibited in their design. But an irritated da Vinci grabbed his brush and blotted them both out. "It is not those cups I want you to see," he exclaimed. "It is *that face* . . . the face of Christ!"

And *that face* is what we must see. Until *that face* comes out of the painting, and out of the Bible, and out of the pulpit, and out of our Sunday School material, we will never have that power. Until Jesus, through the Holy Spirit, comes into our life style, there can be no newness in our drab existence. And there will be no successful witnessing.

NOTES

1. Frank Cumbers, ed., *Daily Readings from the Works of Leslie D. Weatherhead* (Nashville: Abingdon Press, 1968), p. 264

Chapter 4

"Try the Un-method"

I attended a soul-winning clinic the other day. Hundreds of kids sat together to learn how to win people to Christ. Speaker after speaker got up to share his technique. One said, "It's all in the approach . . . you either win them or lose them on the first impression."

Another assured everyone it is the attitude. "A good positive attitude will always reap results," he promised.

One rather obese gentleman said it all rests in hard work, "If you talk to enough people, you're going to win some of them."

A pastor said, "The most important thing is to convince them they are sinners . . . then they'll get saved."

I kept waiting for someone to talk about the real spiritual power giver, but they never did.

Finally, all the kids were organized into little groups. Each task force was assigned a specific part of the city to attack. Then a spiritual pep rally was held. The last speaker gave a closing pep address. There was a moment of prayer for the troops . . . and off to battle!

Most of the kids spent the afternoon drinking cokes at the Dairy Queen. A few genuinely shared Christ, but with slim results. Here we are . . . a hugh conference! Fantastic opportunity. Hundreds of kids. Tons of spiritual potential. Lots of spiritual activity . . . but so little, if any, activity of the Spirit.

Why? The church thought it couldn't beat the world so we joined it. We thought it couldn't do better than the ad men and promoters, so we copied them. But we are like the kid who meticulously copies the test paper of a good-looking girl; then finds out when the papers are handed back that she isn't very smart.

"Put out enough effort, speak the right words, flash the right smile, make the right approach, give the right example," we are told, "and it will mean results." "God blesses those who help themselves; if we want a great church, we can have one if we work hard enough," they say. "If you want to win people to Jesus, you can if you try long enough," they tell us.

And sometimes God does bless these methods. Because that's all we offer him, sometimes he produces some harvest from that kind of sowing. I know that from personal experience; I grew up that way, I have been trained that way, I have seen results from methods.

And teaching kids better methods is better than no advice at all. But it is about as close to the key to witnessing as a hairpin is to the key for a school locker. Yes, in the right hands it may work occasionally. But a satisfactory long-range solution to the problem? *Never!*

Witnessing success does not come from better

methods. It comes when the Holy Spirit gets into the life style of Mr. Average Anybody. Did Paul study Madison Avenue approachers as preparation to win Asia Minor? No! Paul studied God through prayer and the Scriptures. Then God, through his Holy Spirit, reshaped Paul's life style into the kind that moves men to Jesus.

"What's wrong with *this system* or *that system* of evangelism?" someone is always asking me. "Isn't it the best method we know of?" But the question is phony. "What's wrong with the system?" It is a system . . . that's what's wrong! And God doesn't use systems to move people toward him (not primarily at least). He uses the Holy Spirit. He finds a man who will open his life so the Holy Spirit can be poured in; then he saturates that man's life style with the Holy Spirit. Then, and only then, does that man become a successful witness.

"Abide in me . . ." Jesus tells us. "As the branch cannot bear fruit by itself, unless it abides in the vine, neither can you, unless you abide in me" (John 15:4). There is the key . . . the Holy Spirit . . . you in Jesus and Jesus in you through the Holy Spirit. The fruit of a Christian is another Christian. And the only way you can bear that fruit is to let him live in you. If you do, the Holy Spirit will give you the conviction that is needed to get the the job done. He will tell you who to witness to, how to witness, and the words to use. Then he will produce in you the greatest joy of being a Christian . . . seeing another man find Jesus too.

"Completely dependent on the Holy Spirit" . . . that is our situation. We *alone* can do nothing. No matter how filled with the latest psychological gimmicks, no matter how many of the "Ten Steps to Become a Great Salesman" we have memorized, we can't do it *alone*. Dressed in our best "Proven Techniques" we are helpless *alone*. And it isn't even a "Do All You Can and Count on Jesus to Do the

Rest" situation. It isn't a "He's My Helper" game. Instead, it is Jesus in complete charge using your mind, your personality, your life, your talents, of which he is boss. When we begin to understand that, Christ will begin to use us.

We drifted into using systems out of sincere motives. Frustrated because we couldn't get people to witness, we decided to "program' them to witness. Perhaps if we can get them to practice witnessing for two hours a week from 7:00 to 9:00 P.M. on Tuesdays, we think, it may influence them to witness the rest of the week. Not so! Just the reverse! Because they have been programed for two hours, they think they have now done their witnessing bit for this week. Thank goodness! they think. Now we don't have to do that again until next week. Actually, what we do in most canned witnessing programs is not witnessing at all; it is visiting. And it has not led us to do more witnessing, but less.

Nobody witnesses until he is motivated by the Holy Spirit. A friend of mine is an example. She used to try so hard to win people because she knew as a Christian, she was suppose to. But many times, she got frustration and failure. Only when she turned loose and let the Holy Spirit do it through her was she filled with power. First, she tried to psyche herself into it. That didn't work because she was trying to use her own strength. The Holy Spirit works because he doesn't depend on her puny power. He was God in her . . . and that's power.

Again, don't misunderstand. I'm not saying, "Throw away all the systems and manuals." Sometimes they can be useful and helpful. They have their place. And a good system can bring you many annual additions to the church. But systems *alone* aren't enough. If a system is all you depend on, you will continue to be a boldless witness in a day of boldness.

Have you ever noticed how quickly a new Christian wins others to Jesus? He does it so naturally. You almost have to teach him how "not to witness" to keep him from it. Like Andrew in the Bible, kids instantly say, "I am going to get my friends so they can get saved too." They say the same about their mothers and fathers, "I want them to get Jesus too."

What happens to this zeal? Where does it go? Why doesn't it last? Could it be like this? Johnny gets into one of our churches. He wants to learn how to witness, so we tell him to come to the Tuesday night visiting program. He shows up a few nights later. Four other people are there. He is given two prospect cards and told his objective is to "get them to join the church." He is told how hard it is to witness. Some dear brother stands up and says, "I have gone visiting for years and I have not seen anyone saved yet, but I am still faithful. I still come every Tuesday night."

Then we tell Johnny to go out and stand at a front door. Objective: To talk to a stranger about church membership. Over and over we tell him not to expect overwhelming results. "God did not tell you to be successful, just faithful," we tell him. "Don't be discouraged if no one is home."

So off he goes. On the way, he passes four drive-in restaurants where there are hundreds of people. He is inclined to stop and tell them about Jesus, but "you can't go up to that prospect's door after 9:00 P.M." So he goes on. At the corner, a car full of kids comes up and he wants to tell them about Jesus. But he has these two prospect cards in his hand, so he hurries on. Finally, he finds the house. He rushes up to the door with great excitement and rings the bell expectantly. And sure enough . . . it happens . . . nothing. The second house is the wrong address. So he drives back to the church to make his report.

"Cheer up," he is told, "it is tough to be a real witness for Jesus." He leaves. His excitement has been cut in half. "But at least you will be able to try to witness again next Tuesday," he thinks to himself.

And it is admirable that people keep doing this week after week . . . the few who do. They are dedicated. They are determined. They are sincere. They are trying. But until witnessing becomes more than just a programed Tuesday evening event . . . until witnessing becomes a life style instead of a weekly toy . . . it won't work.

"Where have all the new Christians gone?" Where are those so eager to win people when they were filled with the fresh excitement of conversion? Why do we get so timid so soon? Why does enthusiasm die so young in Christians? Simple! Because we smother it to death with methods instead of fertilizing it with the Holy Spirit.

An empty coffeepot will not pour. No matter how hard you shake it or where you plug it in, it will not pour. Why do we not pour out witnessing like the early disciples? Because when we are saved, instead of leading us to the power of the Holy Spirit, somebody sticks a method in our hand.

"And do not get drunk with wine . . . but be filled with the Spirit" Paul said (Eph. 5:18). There are other things we can be filled with that will do as much damage as wine. Paul didn't say it, but I wish he had, "Do not get drunk with techniques, programs, etc., but be filled with the Holy Spirit."

We have a new trinity these days . . . God, the Father; Christ, the Son; and the manual the holy method. But it's a poor substitute. It doesn't complete the triangle. So the power for witnessing pours out through the gapping hole. "Be filled with the Spirit." Note that he didn't say, "Be filled with the method." Print that on a sign and hang it in the front of your brain . . . "Be filled with the Spirit."

The apostles did not succeed at witnessing until

they caught the Holy Spirit at Pentecost. On that day, three thousand people were added to the church (Acts 2:41). When the disciples went into Samaria, they prayed that the Christians there might receive the Holy Spirit (Acts 8:15–16). When the first missionary journey was planned from Antioch, the Holy Spirit directed Paul and Barnabas to do it (Acts 13:2). Dozens of times in the book of Acts, we see examples of the Holy Spirit directing the witnessing.

Early Christians took the Holy Spirit so seriously that he is mentioned ninety-one times in the New Testament. Jesus even said, "Whoever speaks against the Holy Spirit will not be forgiven, either in this age or in the age to come" (Matt. 12:32). Why this strong statement? Because he is the part of God that works through us. God directed the exodus of the Hebrew nation from Egypt. Jesus directed the work of the apostles before his death. And the Holy Spirit directs the work of witnessing in the church.

The crisis of the modern church is that we have lost the Holy Spirit (or never found it). The first disciples waited in prayer from the day of ascension to Pentecost to get their marching orders from the Holy Spirit. But what do we do? We are hardly willing to wait fifteen minutes for the Holy Spirit to show us his plan! We are more likely to design our own marching orders . . . rush off to the battle . . . and then come home wondering why God wasn't with us today.

We have come a long way since the day of Pentecost. We have built fine buildings, educated our preachers, brought meaningful dignity to our worship services. That's good. But, there has been another growth in the church . . . stagnation, apathy, and tired enthusiasm. Why? We have not sought the Holy Spirit. Any diminishing congregation, in any place, in any age, doesn't have far to look for the reason. A basketball team which loses its spirit is in for a siege of failures. And a church which loses the Holy Spirit is headed for lifelessness and uselessness.

The Quakers could teach us something about the Holy Spirit. I don't know if this is still true, but it used to be: In a Quaker board meeting where an important decision needs to be made, the vote is not taken until all agree. How do they agree? They remain in prayer and silence until they can agree. The Quakers believe that if you pray long enough the Holy Spirit will speak to each person and a consensus will be reached. I am not ready to become a Quaker, but I am ready to say this, "The quiet determination to seek the Holy Spirit is something we witnesses must learn again."

"The rush of a mighty wind" (Acts 2:2): That's how the Holy Spirit is described in the New Testament. And the church *without* the Holy Spirit becomes *nothing but* a mighty rushing wind . . . just a lot of hot air, full of sound and fury and signifying little . . . just a mighty rushing wind of programs that accomplish minor results.

Electrical power is always present in thunderstorms. But it doesn't get anything constructive *done* there. It must be gathered at a power plant and sent through wires to your house. The Holy Spirit is the same. He is always available. But he will never take control until you seek him and open your life to him. He will never open your spiritual mouth and cram himself down your throat. But when you're willing to admit that you totally depend on him in every area of your life . . . then he'll take total charge. When that happens, your witness will become as dynamic as a power station.

For the Spirit-saturated person, witnessing is not an act he does; it is a life style. It is as natural as getting up for breakfast. He shares his personal experiences with Christ so that other people can understand the gospel, realize the need of salvation, and understand how to get saved. He does not think of this as a spectacular *act*, but as a part of the way he lives . . . like what he wears to school or to work.

We see this life style again and again in the Bible. Paul went to the Gentiles (not just on Tuesday evening, but all week). Paul witnessed equally naturally to the common people and to the intellectuals (Acts 17:16–34). Phillip stopped to talk with an Ethiopian who was driving down the street (Acts 8:26–39). Andrew ran immediately to get his brother Peter (probably from a fishing boat) (John 1:40–42). Peter, walking into the Temple, stopped to touch a lame man (Acts 3:1–7). Stephen witnessed to the religious leaders of his town (Acts 6–7). Peter and John spoke before the city council (Acts 4). Barnabas went from city to city with Paul (Acts 14).

This was not a method. It was their life style. They didn't do it because it was their "Christian duty" to witness. Nor did they go because it was their "responsibility as good church members." It was not their sense of service that drove them to it. It was not their right, not their opportunity that impelled them. It was their life! "For me to *live* is Christ," Paul said. (Phil. 1:21).

God has given Paul the secret to share with Christians for eternity . . . for me to live is Christ. Not Christ-like, but Christ. And when he is living your life, then your life style will be his life . . . and Jesus can tell anybody about Jesus better than anyone else. So give your life to Christ. Let him reign as King and Master . . . let him fill you with the Holy Spirit . . . and let him lead, direct and control every area of your witness life style.

40

Chapter 5

"Self-destruct your Ego"

When I entered evangelism, I was determined to give my best. I would work harder and longer than anyone. I would be the best preacher and our team would be the most successful . . . if we died trying. And many times our team would work to complete physical exhaustion because we knew of the lost millions and how desperately God was depending upon us to reach them. And we did . . . our first year in evangelism there were over five thousand decisions made for Christ . . . our second year saw over fourteen thousand decisions registered.

Then one day I heard a man preaching, "God needs you . . . " "God is dependent upon you." God need me? I thought, How totally ridiculous? How could Almighty God need me? Instead of God needing me it was me needing God . . . for in the middle of our success I knew there had to be more than what I had found.

The more I looked at my life, the more I saw the "striving of the flesh." So much of everything I did was centered on the strength of the flesh. It was *me* trying to be the witness! It was *me* trying to be the evangelist! It was *me* trying to be the teacher! It was *me* trying to be the prayer warrior! It was *me* trying to be the Christian!

Oh, I was never so foolish as to go into the pulpit in my own power . . . I knew what power brought them down the aisle, but the areas outside of the pulpit . . . I found myself trying to do my best . . . but not really letting him do it.

Then the Scripture hit me: ". . . all our righteous deeds are as filthy rags." Me, at my very best . . . that's what I was . . . filthy rags! For the first time in my life I realized that *I* alone could do nothing spiritually.

But as I studied further in the Word of God, I found I did not have to do it. I was not expected to do it. Even Jesus could not do it. "The Son can do nothing of his own accord" (John 5:19). So why should I think I could?

Then I realized that I was witnessing because I knew I was supposed to. And when I witnessed, there was no total depending on the Holy Spirit. I knew where to go. I had the Scriptures all marked out and the method down pat. And many times God blessed his gospel as I presented it. Yet, I knew there had to be more to the Christian experience than I had found . . . there had to be more power and more personal victory!

God led me to a man named Jack Taylor. Through him, God led me to an experience called *being filled with the Holy Spirit.* What a difference that has made! Coming after months of searching, it involved a genuine and open confession of sin. Unbelievable was the well of deep unconfessed sin I found in my life. Next came a specific claiming of death to self (choosing against my own desires in every area of life . . . self-destructing my ego).

That sounded simple at first, so, I started throwing areas of my life down before the throne of Jesus.

I asked him to do anything he wanted with them. I threw down my home. I threw down my future, my finances, my team, my wife. But finally came my ministry. There was a pause . . . what if he did not want to do with my ministry what I wanted to do with it? How foolish . . . I was willing to trust him with every area of my life . . . except my ministry.

But over and over the echo came back, "Without me you can do nothing. That which is of the flesh is flesh" (John 3:6). So with a sigh of Christian relief, I gave it. That most cherished possession . . my ministry . . . it now belonged totally to Jesus.

Since then, numbers and statistics have become tools instead of "ends." They have become things of joy instead of means to *pride*. I no longer need to depend upon my cunning or wisdom as a soul-winner. For, now, instead of being *my* brilliance, it is his! Instead of being *my* wisdom, it is his! Instead of being *my* persuasiveness, it is his! Instead of being *my* knowledge, it is his! He is in charge; I am to be his tool.

It no longer matters what people say when I share Jesus with them. My name and reputation and prestige are no longer on the line; they are in the hands of God. Jesus puts himself on the line, and he's already won the battle!

I do not say that this is a once-in-a-lifetime experience. I do not claim that all ego temptation is ended. I still feel the need Paul felt . . . to die daily so Jesus can live and witness through me (1 Cor. 15:31). But being filled with the Holy Spirit has freed me from my frightened, revolting dependence on self. And what a joy that is.

None of us like to admit that we are egotistical.

We like to endorse that trait over to other people. But we are all in bondage to some degree . . . to our self-assertive self, our ego, our pride.

Someone asked a famous orchestra conductor

which instrument is the hardest to play. The maestro thought a moment and said, "Second fiddle. I can get plenty of first violinists, but to find someone who plays second fiddle with enthusiasm . . . that is a big problem." Nobody wants to play second fiddle in anything. We all want to be first. We want to move our self-assertive self to center stage. We want others to look at us . . . to see our skill and our accomplishments.

But until you humble yourself to the Father and give him total charge of your life, nothing will happen. If your highest goal is to make the big impression, you will foul out as a witness. If the big thing in your life is to be popular in school . . . the football star, the homecoming queen, have the hot car . . . that means Jesus will have to take second place and you will be a powerless witness. He doesn't care to just be a part of your bag . . . he demands to be King!

Driving to San Antonio I listened to the report of the astronauts coming down after a ten-day trip. Just at a crucial moment I went under a long steel bridge. As usual, my radio communication went off until I got to the other side. Our pride and ego does the same to God. It jams the airways. It builds a barrier so we can't get God's message.

And if we Christians find that our primary concern is a seat at the head table, God's presence will elude us. Pride and God are like positive and negative magnets. They will not occupy space in the same man. A God who humbled himself to wash feet will not live in a heart filled with ego.

If your primary interest is to become a better teacher than someone else . . . to become a better choir member than someone else . . . to become a better pianist than someone else . . . to become a better preacher than someone else . . . then you are merely pursuing the pagan construction of your own ego. Nothing has really changed about your basic selfishness. You are using another gimmick to help you to feel better about yourself.

A woman once said to E. Stanley Jones, "I've found you out. You have only one remedy for every problem . . . self-surrender."

Jones laughed and said: "I'm glad you found me out for I had found myself out. I cannot go down any road with anybody on any problem without running into the necessity of self-surrender. Your self on your hands is a problem and a pain. Your self in the hands of God is a possibility and a power."[1]

Right! If you want God to touch others through you, go and sell what you have (whatever occupies the selfish center of your life) and come, follow Christ.

Don't get hung up at this point . . . this is what it means to commit ego suicide. Just suppose you could lay down in a coffin and die and as soon as you were dead Jesus would come get into your body and live his life inside your body. That would be great . . . fantastic! In essence, that's what he wants. Of course, you cannot physically die, but you can choose death in the area of sin and rebellion against God . . . and you can choose to let Jesus come alive through the Holy Spirit in your life. You can become a body and a mind and a personality whose very life is Jesus. He wants to become your thoughts . . . your motivation . . . your love . . . your life.

Sinless perfection . . . no! The things you don't want to do you still do . . . because Satan hates Jesus and tries to destroy everything he owns. But power and victory . . . yes! Because he's overcome the world! Praise Jesus! HALLELUJAH!

NOTES

1. Stanley Jones, *A Song of Ascents* (Nashville: Abingdon, 1968), p. 230.

Chapter 6

"One Raised to the Highest Power"

One evening after a backyard barbecue, I returned to be sure the fire was out. It wasn't. But as I held my hand close to the charcoal, I could feel no heat. Then I poked at a briquette with a stick. To my amazement, it fell to pieces. The little piles of cold ashes had held their original wagon wheel shape. But the fire was gone.

Remind you of anything? A layman said to me: "I joined the church twenty years ago. It was a great experience. Now I attend every week. I even hold an office and teach a Sunday School class. But I haven't talked with anyone about Jesus in years. What's the matter with me?" That describes a lot of us. The fire of enthusiasm is extinguished. Oh, the shape is still there, but the excitement is gone.

Has that happened to you? Do you have a constant feeling of spiritual "low house power"? If you have, I'm sure you want to ask: "What can I do about it? How can I get back the witnessing power of a new Christian? How do I keep it after I get it?"

The first step is to believe that God's Holy Spirit

really does exist. You must believe that your car is parked in front of your house before you can get into it. You must believe that you have a stove in your kitchen before you can cook dinner on it. I must believe that you, the reader, exist. Otherwise, I would not write this book. You must believe this book exists. Otherwise, you would never try to read it.

Many of us haven't made that basic decision to *believe* in the Holy Spirit. We have decided to believe in lots of other things we can't see and understand. We believe in radio waves that pass invisibly through the air. We believe in electrical impulses that pass over telephone cables. We believe in television signals. We even believe in E.S.P. and horoscopes and the prophetic powers of Jeane Dixon. But most of us still don't really believe in God's Spirit. Why? We are afraid. That idea sounds too unscientific!

Like radio waves, the Holy Spirit is always available. He can be released to anyone at any time. Tune in your receiving equipment to the proper wavelength and you get his transmission into your life. I don't pretend to understand how this works. But I know it does.

There is a wavelength of God. There is TV, shortwave, FM, and AM. But there is a more important one. We might call it GM. And all you have to do is turn on and tune in to it. But most of us don't.

A friend of mine runs an accounting firm that does business all over the United States. When they ordered a new $150,000 computer, the company shipped all the parts for it except the plug-in cords. There they were with a $150,000 piece of equipment that they couldn't plug in. That is where many of us are with the power of God. We have the delicate electronics of the human mind, the human spirit, the human emotions (much more intricate than the computer), but we can't get it plugged in.

We think of infinity as the biggest possible number, the highest possible power. But it isn't. A far greater power is one person raised to the power of the Holy Spirit. His is the greatest power in the universe.

"But I can't witness! I'm just not good at that sort of thing," you say. You don't have to be good at it. *Jesus is!* God doesn't depend on your talent anyway. He is smarter than that. But with the Holy Spirit you go to witness, not just in your power, but in God's power.

"Go therefore. . . ." Christ said (Matt. 28:19). But wait! He didn't say, "Go on your own strength." He knew that would never be enough. He said, "I am with you always, even to the close of the age." (Matt. 28:20).

Why did the church at Antioch grow? Certainly not because of their own power; not because they had a great new gimmick or a good mimeograph machine. It grew because common men with no religious training let the Holy Spirit lead them. And that describes the laymen in every rapidly growing church in America. They give themselves to Jesus, and let him raise them to the highest power.

Jesus came along one day and found the disciples fishing. "Children, have you any fish?" He asked.

"No," they replied.

"Cast the net on the right side of the boat, and you will find some," he told them. So they cast it there, and then they were not able to haul it in; it was too full (John 21:5–6). That is the way with our witnessing. Without Jesus, through the Holy Spirit, we may fish with the latest techniques, but we won't catch much. That's because God isn't in it; just us.

God promised us this power centuries before Christ came. God said to the prophet, Joel: "And it shall come to pass afterward, that I will pour out my spirit on all flesh; . . . Even upon the man-servants and maidservants in those days, I will pour out my spirit" (Joel 2:28–29).

At Pentecost this came true. God poured out his Spirit on ordinary men and women. Through this Spirit, he gave them power to live new lives . . . to do new things that they could never do before. And it is happening again today. All around us, it is happening.

You may say, "How does Jesus raise us to this higher power in witnessing?"

Through a commitment of your mind. Then he controls your thought impulses. (The devil will never give you the mental and spiritual desire to tell someone about Jesus. Only the Holy Spirit does that.) All you do is see the person through the eyes of Jesus and allow God's love and compassion to flow through you as God leads you to think of their need to know Jesus. You simply trust God to give you the words. They'll come. God always knows what so say. He never has stage fright.

The big question is, Will you let it happen to you? Or, will you run away from it and refuse to let God use you?

What happens to a Christian if he does not let the Holy Spirit contact? Well, what did Jesus say about the branches that do not bear fruit? Right, he said they are cut off (John 15:6). What does that mean . . . that once you are saved, you are lost. No! It simply means that you are put on the side lines. You are set on the shelf. Instead of being in the action part of the Kingdom, you are stuck on the bench.

When I was a junior in high school our football team won the state championship. . . . but I hardly got to play at all. My leg was in a cast. The coach put me in for the last ten seconds of the game. I didn't get to be in even one play. Yes, I lettered that year because I had played in so many of the other

games. And on my jacket was a patch for state champions. But it didn't mean a lot. The next year we won state also. But that patch means a lot more. Why? I didn't sit on the bench and watch. I got to be in there where the action really happened.

Many see the Christian life as boring and dry. It is for some people. You come to church . . . you sit . . . listen . . . it doesn't mean anything. Why aren't you excited? Because you are a bench-warming branch that's not bearing fruit. No wonder it is dull! How could it be otherwise?

I'll never forget an event during my first year in evangelism. I was in Oklahoma City getting ready to go into the service. A young lady came running up to me shouting, "He's here, he's here."

I looked at her a little strangely and said, "Who's here?"

"An atheist in my science class at Central State

University," she said. "Oh, preacher, if you could win him to Jesus, you could win anyone to Christ."

I assured her that I'd preach as well as possible and told her to go and pray.

As I entered the service, Darcie Hodges was already singing. About ten minutes later this guy walked in the back door. He had long hair, Jesus-sandals, shirt-tail hanging out, and Winstons in his left pocket.

When he walked in that door, two deacons keeled over. Another one, made out of stronger stuff, said, "Would you look at that . . . a real live sinner in our church." (They hadn't seen one of those in so long they didn't know what to do with him.)

Down the aisle he came and sat on about the fourth seat back. I thought to myself, He doesn't know it, but he's in range. I preached to him harder than I've ever preached. I just knew he'd come running down the aisle and give his life to Jesus.

But not so! In the invitation, he folded his arms and looked at me as if to say, "Well, man, you sure didn't impress me."

When the service was over, he went walking out and I thought I'd never see him again.

But on Thursday night he was back, and I preached on the second coming of Jesus. When I gave the invitation that night, he was the first one down the aisle. Oh, he didn't come to get saved. He came to tell me how completely "out of it" I was.

So I took him in the counseling area and gave him to a brilliant young Ph.D. from the University of Oklahoma. They spent about forty minutes together until the professor finally just gave up and turned him back over to me.

As soon as I walked into the room to talk with him, he propped his feet up on the table and said, "Preacher, this is the biggest bunch of junk I've ever heard." He said, "I don't believe one single word of this stuff."

So we started talking. We went through everything . . . history . . . philosophy . . . ideology . . . authenticity . . . the whole bit!

Finally I said, "If there really is a God would you like to know him?"

He said, "Sure, if there really is a God, I'd like to know him."

I said, "OK, let's pray. Ask God if he does exist to reveal himself to you."

"That's ridiculous!" he replied.

I said, "Well, probably so, but let's try it anyway."

"Well, if it'll make you happy," he replied.

"There's nothing to lose, is there?" I asked him. "So, let's try it."

So he prayed, "God, I don't know who you are. In fact, I don't even know if you are. But if you are, reveal yourself to me." After that, he got up and left.

About two weeks later I was back in Oklahoma City when he came again. At the invitation he came walking down the aisle. Striding right up to the pulpit, he said, "Preacher, I'm ready."

I said, "Ready for what?"

"I'm ready to give my life to Jesus," he said.

"Great," I said, "But why? What changed your mind?"

He replied, "You know all those things you told me about Jesus being an actual historical person who really lived . . . was a religious zealot . . . had a group of disciples . . . was crucified . . . and whose body was mysteriously missing the third day? Well, I've been living in libraries since then. And I proved that for myself. That's all *the basis for my faith* I need. I'm ready to really turn my life over to Jesus." So right there, we prayed and he became a Christian.

I had preached that night on crowns. I told the people that every time you lead someone to Christ, that at the judgement seat of Christ you'll be given a crown of joy (1 Thess. 2:19).

As soon as he got saved he said, "Preacher, were you shooting straight about those crowns?"

"Sure," I said.

"What are you going to do with all those crowns?" he countered.

"Well, in the middle of our receiving all those crowns, we will get to take all of them and lay them at the feet of Jesus when he is crowned King of kings," I said. "And I hope I have so many crowns that I have to say, 'Pull up the Illinois Central and load her up.'"

He turned away and said, "I'm going to get me some crowns."

The next night he was back with a friend. As soon as I gave the invitation, he came walking down the aisle with his friend. He looked me right in the eye and said, "Preacher, that's one." And for the next thirteen nights he led someone to faith in Jesus.

Here was a young man who was as atheistic as you can be. But today he's one of the most outstanding Christians I've ever met. He literally wins thousands of people to Jesus every year. His name is Bill Landers. He's the director and composer of the Jesus rock group "Three-In-One."

You talk about Christianity becoming exciting. There's nothing in the world as exciting as leading a person to Jesus and seeing Christ change his life.

If you are not enjoying your relationship with the Lord, it's probably because you are not touching someone else with Jesus and watching his power work to make him a new person.

That's what the Jesus touch is all about. If you are touched by committing your life unto Christ, then you will naturally reach out and touch others who are looking in every direction for the purpose and meaning which only comes with the Jesus touch.

Chapter 7

"Meet the Real Silent Majority"

"You sure can offend people with all this 'saved' junk. I just let my Christian example influence people. That's my witness," she said.

About nineteen, long blond hair, sharp clothes, she has a genuine love for Jesus. But she believes a lie. From her elementary years in the church she has been told: "Win people by the example of your life. People can look at you and tell there's a difference. Let others see Jesus in you." And she believes it. She bought it before she unwrapped it.

And she is a sharp girl. Her skirt is not too short. Her neckline is not too low. Her hair is neat. Her breath doesn't smell like smoke. Her language is in no way wrong. She is nice, neat, beautiful, clean, moral, a polished example . . . the ultimate in Christian perfection. But does she lead people to Jesus? Never!

Let's recover from our foggy hallucination! Where would the Coca-Cola Company be if it depended on its superior product *alone?* It would be broke! The

Coke company knows that if you don't advertise, you die a quick, unprofitable death. Where would General Motors be if it did not tell people that it believes in its automobiles? And where would Christianity be if Paul and Barnabas had not *talked with people* in Asia Minor.

Look closer at that little phrase, "I just try to live so people can see my example." It may make us feel better about our silence. But it is a flat untruth. It won't stand the test of the Bible. It flunks the reality exam. And it certainly won't pass with the Holy Spirit. People who are full of Jesus do more than just look like their faith; they talk like it. Andrew *spoke* to his brother, Peter, and brought him to Jesus. Phillip *spoke* to the Ethiopian. Peter *spoke* at Pentecost and saw three thousand baptized. Paul *spoke* to his jailer.

Look at Peter and John in the fourth chapter of Acts. How did they get thrown in jail? Not from living a good moral life. It was because they were telling people about Jesus. The authorities would have happily said: "Look, you two, let people see Jesus in you all you want, but keep your mouth shut about it." No, Peter and John were not concerned about "living it away." They were out to "give it away."

"You shall be my witnesses," Jesus said. Can we be silent witnesses? Imagine a silent witness in court. The case would be thrown out immediately. Imagine a silent car salesman. Imagine a silent store clerk. Imagine a silent TV announcer. Likewise, a silent witness for Christ is no witness at all. True, words not backed up by our lives are meaningless, but a testimony without words is like faith without works . . . DEAD!

Someone is always wondering, "Why are some denominations growing so rapidly while many others are dying out statistically?" The answer is so simple, but many miss it. It isn't their emotionalism. It isn't their ultra-simplistic faith. They talk with people. While some try to win them by shining examples, they talk. While others do social work, they do mouth-to-ear resuscitation.

Everyone else in this world . . . materialistic philosophers, nationalists, intellectualists, racists, Communists . . . they all push their products hard. How? Not by exemplary living. They push them verbally. And they are succeeding in places where we are failing. Why? They know the truth about conversion. You don't win people to any cause just by being a "nice guy."

For years, Henry Ford refused to make a car in any color except black. Because of this, there was a brief period when Ford slid into financial trouble. But he was smart enough not to keep on pursuing a policy that didn't work. He quickly stepped into colors on cars and out of the red on the account books. That is where we Christians are. We blindly insist it is not necessary to talk with people about our faith! No wonder we are in red ink on our roll books!

The other day I read a very sophisticated article on "The Communications Gap in Evangelism." The article charged that we have a terminology problem in witnessing. "Non-Christians do not understand us, and thus, reject the gospel," it said. But it missed the real problem. We do have a communications problem, right! But the gap is not where we think it is. It is certainly not in the kind of language we use. The gap is created because we use *no language at all*.

Sure, we communicate with each other, perhaps over-communicate, but not with non-Christians. We seldom talk with them at all. We are the "silent majority!"

A little girl wrote home to her father from summer vacation: "Dear Daddy, Hi! I don't really have much to say." That describes our current communication with the world. "Hi! I don't really have much to say."

Almost any kind of terminology will work to some degree in witnessing. But nothing will work unless you actually say something.

We got a letter in the office the other day informing us of a coming event. It was obviously wrong, however. The date called for Wednesday being on the seventh of the month. This isn't the case . . . not this year at least. It was also clear that the writer could not spell. What a mess it was! But our secretary, who always looks for the positive in people, said, "Well, at least he took the time to write."

Many religious radicals are inaccurate with their information about God. They are often impolite and unsophisticated in their presentation. But at least they come to your door. That is something many of us don't do. We want them to get the message about Christ, but we never take time to write. Why then should we expect to communicate with anyone? Why then should we expect good statistical results?

Let's bury the old "silence myth" forever. So what if her skirt is an inch longer. Most people don't carry a yardstick anyway. So she would win the "Gladys Good Breath Award." Most people don't get that close. So her life is great. So are the lives of thousands who have never accepted Christ. But do they influence others toward Jesus?

It is Satan who tells us we can win people to Jesus by living a good life. Look around! There are more Christians in the world than ever before, more churches than ever before. There are more "Jesus Saves" highway signs than ever. But we are not reaching them. Why? Because we are following

Jesus' patterns in every way except one . . . telling people about him.

Thousands wear the right clothes, smile the right smiles, use the right language, attend the right services. But where is the person who talks about Jesus? He has become the Christian stranger . . . a part of the vocal minority. In fact, he's so strange that many Christians are usually suspicious of him. Fine, be different from the world! But unless the world knows what makes you different, they'll never find Jesus.

Don't get me wrong. We should be living good moral lives. We should be inwardly and outwardly clean. Paul says, "If any one purifies himself from what is ignoble, then he will be a vessel for noble use, consecrated and useful to the master" (2 Tim. 2:21). To be useful, your life must be clean. Paul says to the Romans, "Present your bodies a living sacrifice, holy, acceptable unto God, which is your reasonable service." (Rom. 12:1, KJV)

Yes, the result of being saved is living like it. Talking about Christ will be a job if others can't "see" the difference He makes in the way you live. But, an effective witness must be a combination of two aspects: living and giving Christ. One without the other will not go far or last long.

Imagine, if you can, Paul and Barnabas talking together in Antioch. They are laying plans for the evangelization of Asia Minor. Paul says to Barnabas, "Now Barnabas, I have a plan. Here is what we are going to do. We are going to settle down here in Antioch. We will live such a great Christian life that people will come from all over to join our church. Soon the Christian faith will spread all the way to Rome." Ridiculous, isn't it? But what are we doing?

It is not by accident that the gospel is called the *good news*. (Note that it is not called the good example or the good way.) It is not by accident that

John says, "And the *Word* became flesh and dwelt among us" (John 1:14). The word became flesh . . . The *word* (Jesus) was God in the flesh, openly revealing himself to man. He didn't come as an example of God. He came to do what only God could do . . . die for our sins. It was not his good life and example that saves us. It was his death. He openly acted as the Word of God.

And when you are filled with the Word (by turning your life over to Jesus), that *Word* (Jesus) is going to openly *tell* other people how they can be saved. This is the way God has always worked. He *became* the words of the prophets. He *became* the words of the apostles. And he *becomes* the words of Christians today as they share with people what he has done to set them free. And our witness will never get the job done until we use words to tell the world about Jesus, "The Word."

Over in Arizona, there is a man who runs a dry cleaners. For five years he did the cleaning for nineteen ministers and countless laymen. Yet not one of them ever told him about Jesus. Today he is a Christian. He is active in the church; a tither. Why? Because one of his customers finally started using words instead of the excellent example of his Christian life.

Chapter 8

"Get your Signals Straight"

"Don't give me this 'saved' stuff. What are you talking about anyway?" responded a frustrated young soldier.

The teen-ager continued his efforts: "But wait a minute. I'm talking about Jesus, you know, the Son of God. Have you ever really turned your life over to him?"

"Oh, yeh," the soldier replied, obviously relieved to talk about something he understood, "I'm a Christian. I used to go to church all the time. My parents still do."

"Great!" the young evangelist replied. "That's all I really wanted to know."

In baseball, the pitcher who constantly misreads the catcher's signals floats the old ball game down the sewer. That's us! Many times we communicate dedicated confusion when we witness. Jesus, through the New Testament, gives us some plain signals. But we immediately muddle them up so we never get down to the real issues.

How do you become a Christian? We know a person ought to be one, but we don't know how to tell someone the directions for getting there. We confuse it with church membership, with believing in God, with having a family Bible, getting baptized, going through catechism, and a thousand other things.

Halford Luccock told a story about a New England farmer who shingled his house one foggy day. But he got careless. He came to the roof's edge and shingled right off into the fog.

There are several reasons for this confusion. Two of them are worth discussing before we go on to deal with the signals that Jesus gives.

The first is our current kick for "religious tolerance" in this country. Two Hollywood actresses were discussing their horoscopes. One said to her friend, "I didn't know you believed in astrology?"

Her friend replied, "Oh, yes, I believe in everything a little bit." That's us! We believe in everything a little bit. We tend to tolerate all religious ideas. We label this tolerance a virtue. It isn't.

A county agent tells about a man who came into his office one day lugging a big sack of dirt. "Where can I get my soil samples tested?" he asked.

You take soil samples for nutrient testing by going all over a field. You gather paper sacks of dirt from numerous locations. Then you draw a map showing the chemist where you got the samples. But this man had obviously brought all his samples in one big sack. So, the county agent asked, "Uh, by the way, how did you take your soil samples?"

The farmer replied, "Well, I just waited for a rainy day, drove the tractor all over the farm, then cleaned the dirt off the tires."

That accurately describes the religious thinking of many Americans. We drive all around, take a little bit of this, a little bit of that, dump it all in a sack, and call it "our faith."

Don't misread me. I'm not kicking the Christian virtue of tolerance. Let the various denominations attempt to understand each other. The Spanish Inquisition and European religious wars amply illustrate the faults of narrow-mindedness. Our directions to "Live in harmony with one another" (Rom. 12:16) demand something better than our forefathers practiced.

But if you push the tolerance fad too far, it drags you over a cliff. We cannot tolerate violent men in our streets in the name of tolerance. We cannot tolerate lawlessness in our society in the name of tolerance. And we cannot tolerate the idea that "A man's religion is his own business. I should not try to win him to Christ." That's certainly not the wish of Jesus.

Don't misunderstand the nature of Christian tolerance. Paul does not say anywhere that we should learn to tolerate the untruths of paganism. No! Paul would not tolerate anything that did not have Christ at the core. Why did he wring out his life traveling around preaching? He was convinced that unless a man lets Jesus take over as Lord and Savior he never finds what life is all about. And, if he dies without Jesus, he would spend eternity in hell separated from God. Paul didn't call for toleration but for conversion.

Samuel Butler said: "An open mind is all very well, but it ought not to be so open that there is no keeping anything in or out of it." Many religious minds are open at both ends. Like a sieve, they take in everything but hold onto nothing. Don't confuse open-mindedness and empty-headedness!

Jesus meant it when he said: "I am the way, and the truth, and the life; no one comes to the Father, but by me" (John 14:6). That is why he sent the seventy out (Luke 10:1–22) not to tolerate the world, but to change the world. That's why he called the twelve . . . not to tolerate the world's ideas, but to change the world's ideas. Did he tell them, "Go into all the world, and *tolerate* everything?" No, he told them to go into all the world and teach what he taught (Matt. 28:19–20).

A second cause of our foggy confusion is the current fad for "substitution." We attempt solutions to our personal problems by substituting methods *other than Jesus*. Two major substitutions are presently in vogue. One is the psychological (understanding and insight into internal hang-ups can make you happy). The other is environmental (examination and improvement of oppressive external circumstances can make you happy). Both are blind alleys. Neither one (though both may be helpful at times) of these answers is real. Neither produces the new life we are all looking for.

Paul tells the Corinthians that the Jews demand miracles, and the Greeks want a philosophical explanation of things, but he preaches Christ (Paraphrase, 1 Cor. 1:23). Paul knew that substituting raw emotionalism *alone* (whether in a brush arbor revival or a psychiatrist's office) doesn't get the job done. Nor does philosophical, well-educated intellectualism *alone* get the job done. Let's get it straight. Jesus is the only solution to the problems this world, our country, and individuals are facing. We need to quit apologizing for that fact and get busy doing what Jesus told us to do.

Now, back to our signals. A young man in Anaheim, California, came up to me one night after the service and asked, "Preacher, what do you tell a person to do if he wants to be saved?" Perhaps the answer I gave him will illustrate what I mean by "getting your signals straight."

"Take your Bible," I said, "And tell him these four things: First, 'All have sinned and fall short of the glory of God' (Rom. 3:23). In other words, man, we're all on our own ego trip. We've set Christ out in the street. Because of this, our life has filled up with junk . . . sin, lust, pride, envy, lying, stealing, adultery . . . all those things that are direct opposites of God. So," I said, "just ask your friend to take a look at his life and ask himself who is on the throne of it; himself or Christ? You won't have to tell him the answer to that. He knows!

"Secondly, have your friend turn in the Bible to Romans 6:23: 'For the wages of sin is death, but the free gift of God is eternal life in Christ Jesus our Lord.' Have him take a close look at that. 'The wages of sin is death!' What is God talking about here?"

"But doesn't everybody die, preacher?" the young man countered.

"Yes, physically everybody dies," I replied. "But that's not what Paul means. Look closer! What is sin, physical or spiritual?"

"Well, as he studied a moment, "spiritual, I guess."

"Right! Sin produces many physical end-results, but sin is basically spiritual. Sin is electing self as chairman of the board of your life. Only God has a right to that position. Since sin is spiritual, so is the death it brings; spiritual death. The Bible calls it hell! Because of our sin, we are all separated from God in a place called hell. Is that right?" I said.

"Yes, but preacher, what about Jesus paying for our sin?" he asked.

"That's where the rest of the verse comes in. 'The gift of God is eternal life through Jesus Christ our Lord.' We all deserve to die and go straight to hell on a fast jet . . . because we've all sinned.

"But God wants to give you a free gift . . . forgiveness for your sin. You don't deserve the gift, but God wants you to have it anyway. Notice, though, it is a gift *through* Jesus Christ. It does not say you get this gift by joining the church or by going

through confirmation class. Nor does it say you get it by being a good person or by giving up all pleasures. You only get it through Jesus.

"We moderns parade our pride in the Reformation of Luther. We brag about our escape from the theological mistakes of the Middle Ages. But we often miss the basic lesson of the Protestant Reformation . . . new life does not come by any kind of working at it, no matter how sincere. We do not earn our salvation; we get it through Christ."

Recalling an old story, I passed it on to him. "A young man once came to a minister saying that he wanted to help build the kingdom of God. The minister asked the boy where in the Bible he found that idea?

"'Well, it may not be said specifically,' the boy replied, 'But surely it is implied.'

"The minister responded unexpectedly, 'Not so! We don't *build* the Kingdom! We *enter* it! We don't establish it; we enter it. And we enter it by sealing the center of our life to Christ. There is no other way.'"

"But why? Why can we get salvation *only* through Jesus?" my young friend continued.

"Remember that sin's price is death . . . *spiritual* death. Jesus paid that price, and only Jesus. When Jesus died on the cross, he not only died a physical death; he also died a spiritual death. 'It was about the ninth hour,' the Bible says, when Jesus cried out, 'My God, my God, why hast thou forsaken me?' (Mark 15:34).

"We easily miss the meaning of this despairing scream. For the first time in history God, the Father, and the Son are separated! Jesus became guilty . . . not of *his sin*, but of *ours*, and the sentence is paid . . . DEATH! Jesus experienced hell on the cross; separation from the Father! He's the only one who ever went through that experience and came out victorious, more alive than ever!

"Now, here's what we've got:

1. Man is a sinner.
2. The wages of sin is death.
3. Jesus has paid the price of our sin.

"Or, you might look at it this way:

1. You are a sinner (on your own ego trip, trying to be God).

2. The salary for this trip is death (eternal separation from God).
3. Jesus has stopped payment on the salary check (with his death on the cross)."

"I finally understand it," the boy said, delighted with his new insight. "But now what do I do after I tell him that?"

"There's only one thing left. Tell your friend how to receive that gift of salvation that God wants to give him," I said. "To do that turn to Romans 10: 9–10. '. . . if you confess with your lips that Jesus is Lord. . . .' Then ask your friend this:

'Do you believe that Jesus is the Son of God?'
'Do you believe that Jesus died on the cross?'
'Do you believe that Jesus was raised from the dead?'

"If he answers yes on these three questions, then read the next phrase, '. . . and believe in your heart that God raised him from the dead. . . .' *Notice* it says believe in your *heart!* What did God mean? Believe in your *blood pumper?*

"Surely if God really put man together, he knows we believe with our *brain!* Of course he does. But God makes one of the biggest points in the Bible with this five-letter word . . . heart. The belief that leads us to salvation is not a mental acceptance of a list of facts; it is the commitment of our very *lives. Believe in your heart!* . . . the real you, not some mental facade that you can hang up or take down like curtains. The Greek word for 'believe' puts it more clearly. It means action . . . a word of 'commit*ment.*'"

"OK, preacher, suppose my friend says he really does believe in Jesus. What now?"

"Ask him this, 'Have you ever really turned your life over to Jesus and accepted him as Lord and

Savior?' That's what believing with your heart is all about. Many people think that, if they are baptized and do their best, they are saved. That isn't true.

"How did Peter become a Christian? Was it because he memorized some great theological beliefs? Was it because he gained some great psychological insights into himself? Was it because he took a long course in the beliefs of the church? No! It was because Jesus said to Peter, 'Follow me!' (Matt. 4:19) And that's what Peter did . . . he followed . . . he let Jesus take charge.

"You are not saved until you make Christ 'managing director' of your life. You can believe in Jesus yet never receive him as Lord. 'Even the demons believe—and shudder,' the Bible reminds us (Jas 2:19). But they sure aren't saved. So explain to your friend that believing 'with the heart' means a real 'commit*ment*' of his life.

"And here's the way you do that: 'Everyone who calls upon the name of the Lord will be saved.' (Rom. 10:13) Here it is:

> everyone . . . anybody (your friend included)
> who calls upon . . . prayer (that's the way we talk with God)
> the name of the Lord . . . *Lord,* that's the key; it means boss, master, owner . . . (that's what Jesus wants)
> will be saved . . . promise (God says he will do it).

So just ask your friend if he's willing to turn things over to Jesus, not just to add Jesus to his bag but really let Jesus be his bag. If he is willing, then have him pray this prayer:

> 'Dear Father, come into my life . . . forgive me of my sin . . . I turn my life entirely over to you, and I receive Jesus Christ as the Lord and Savior of my life . . . Father, you promised

to save me if I asked you to, so, right now I ask you to save me and make me a Christian, and I thank you for doing it . . . in Jesus' name. Amen.'

"Then, as his head is bowed and his eyes are closed, tell him this, 'I promise you on the authority of the Word of God that if you really meant that prayer, you've just been saved. Now, if you really mean it, if you know by faith you really turned your life over to Jesus, reach out here and take my hand.' (The hand has nothing to do with making him a Christian: it's just a way for him to express what's happened in his heart.)

"Have you got it?" I said to the young Californian.

"Yeah, I've got it, but I've got one last question," he said, "What if he's already a Christian?"

"Great," I said, "If he is, teach him what I just taught you!"

Chapter 9

"Jesus Didn't Sit Around"

"You tell us to get into the world," a devout layman said. "But aren't we supposed to stay apart from the world?" To prove his point, he quoted Paul, "Do not be conformed to this world" (Rom. 12:2).

The question was sincere, but it floats past Paul's main point. Paul does not tell us to stay out of the world. He tells us to invade the world. And how can you launch an invasion if you refuse to walk in the sand on the beach?

Let me illustrate. I was going to preach in a crusade the other day. We had just deplaned from a DC-9 and were riding in a new station wagon. We were coming up over a hill doing about sixty, and right in front of us appeared a wagon pulled by a mule. It was full of guys with black hats, black suits, and black pants. They all wore white shirts and black ties. Why? Because they have "set themselves apart from the world."

Now I have every respect for their right to this

life style. But by attempting to avoid conformity to the world, they have moved completely out of the world! They are witnessing drop-outs. Does anyone in our society listen to their witness? No, people just drive around and laugh.

Yes, we are called to be "peculiar people" for Christ (Titus 2:14, KJV). But what does that mean? It does not mean "peculiar" in what we wear or how we look. It means "peculiar" because we have sold out to Jesus Christ.

Take another look at Jesus. How did he dress? Yes, John the Baptist dressed differently. John wore camel's hair and a leather girdle. (Sounds a little like a hippie.) He ate locusts and wild honey. (Now there is a life style that is way out!) But now look at Jesus. No place do we read that he dressed differently from his local culture. Yes, he was different! But the difference was not his clothing; it was what he was.

Yes, we must be careful not to let the world win us. Don't let the food season the salt, or the darkness put out your light. That was the concern of the man who opened this chapter. And it is a good concern. How do you get into the world without letting the world get into you? The prodigal son got into the gutter, but the gutter got into him. He ended up in a pigpen. Our job is to get into the gutter without letting that happen. How to do it?

Same answer, second verse! By keeping in touch with the Spirit. How did Jesus do it? How did Paul do it? Right! By the power of the Spirit . . . by a firmly welded link with the Father. And you can do the same.

Jesus did not sit in his carpenter shop preaching sermons about the hellish conditions in Jerusalem. No! The opposite! He got down to where the world lives.

Jesus did not spend all his time in Bible study groups. Jesus got down into the dirt. He went out where he could "touch" a leper! He picked up mud and put it in a blind man's eyes. He picked up a stick and wrote in the dust to a prostitute.

Yes, we should have all the spiritual prayer time we want. We should attend all the Bible study meetings we care to. Memorize Scripture passages. Be in prayer meeting every Wednesday. But if you do not get your witness out into the common world, you are not doing what Jesus did.

Be the "light of the world," Jesus tells us (Matt. 5:14). Can you be a light if you never leave the bulb factory? Be the "salt of the earth," Jesus said (Matt. 5:13). Can you be salt if you spend all your time in the shaker?

A lot of Christians try to be the "salt of the salt" instead of the "salt of the earth." They want to be the "light of the light" instead of the "light of the world." They never get the body out of the building.

Last summer I saw a fire truck in the ditch. It lay half way over on its side. On top of the truck was a fireman busy spraying water out into a nearby field. You could easily see what had happened. It had just rained. He had turned off the highway on his way to a fire. The side road was unexpectedly slippery. The turn slid him into the ditch. Now he was emptying the truck so it could be pulled out of the ditch. A half mile on down the road you could see the smoke from a burning farm building.

How very like us Christians! The world is so close. It needs Jesus so badly! But we firemen so often fall a half mile short of getting him to where the fire is.

Someone said the first line of a recipe for rabbit stew is "catch a rabbit." But one thing comes before that . . . you must get where the rabbit is before you can catch him.

Witnessing is the act of sharing your *personal experience with Christ*. The person to whom you witness is then able to: 1. Understand the gospel.

2. Realize his need of salvation. 3. Know how to get it. But before that can happen, you must get where that person is.

Remember how we talked about a Christian being an extension cord? And about the need to plug the cord into the wall? Don't make the opposite mistake . . . plug into the wall, but forget to plug into the lamp. That is equally ineffective.

I was helping a man start his car with some battery cables one day. We had all the equipment to do the job. But nothing happened until I actually touched the cables to the battery post. And witnessing doesn't work until you get where people are. You may have a powerful church, a strong preacher, and a lot of high-voltage organization. But nothing will happen until you make contact with someone.

We don't know *how* (the method) Jesus healed the demoniac's troubled mind. We don't know *how* he changed Mary Magdalene into a disciple (what words he used). We don't know *how* he transformed Paul, the Pharisee, into a late-blooming apostle.

But we do know one thing about Jesus' methods. He *wandered about the countryside doing his work,* totally yielded to his father's leadership. You would think that with all his powers . . . with far more to do than he could finish . . . surely he should have set up a clinic. There he could have treated people at maximum efficiency. Surely that would have increased production and reduced energy expenditure! You would think that Jesus would at least have built a building. There, he and his disciples could have lived in comfort while they ministered to the ailing population.

Why didn't he schedule special times when people could come and hear speeches? You would think he would have written a book! But he didn't. Why not? Do you suppose he knew what we haven't learned yet . . . you have to go where people are before you can touch them with God?

Two thousand youth from the Bahai religion recently held a convention at Evanston, Illinois. One of their decisions there was the pledge to increase the spread of their faith. In the next three years, these young people plan to spread the Bahai college clubs from 126 to 200. How will they do this? Not by sitting home.

And can it be true that the Holy Spirit leads young Christians to do less . . . to sit in their churches and wait for drop-in converts? No! We must get in the world!

Chapter 10

"The Jesus Touch"

Asked to call on a new neighbor, a woman replied: "I'd like to, but I just don't have time. I have to decorate the altar at the church. My prayer group meets today too. I have to make some chocolate brownies for it." Another woman said thirteen years passed before she found out where the housekeeper attended church. It turned out that she went to none at all.

These illustrations bring us to a primary character quality of the Christian witness . . . willingness to touch people. And because it is so easily overlooked, it is worth spending a chapter on.

Here again, we get our first clue from Jesus. He didn't spend his ministry reading a book about religion. Nor was he a priest who gave his time to sacrifices on an altar. He was not a scholar whose energies went to questions like, "How many devils can sit on a pinhead?" No! Jesus' primary work was *among people*.

Notice how many times Jesus touched people. He

touched the blind man and made him see. He *touched* the lame man and made him walk. He *touched* the leper and made him whole. (In those days, nobody dared touch a leper, but Jesus did.) And Jesus didn't stop with physical touch. He touched people emotionally and spiritually as well. Remember the Samaritan woman at the well? He stopped in the street to save an adultress from stoning. He called a crooked tax collector down from a tree to go home to dinner with him. Jesus didn't seclude himself in some cozy study. He touched people.

We get our second clue from the apostles. They did not use any of the methods we think so important. They were not writers. They were not scholars. They were not editors of religious journals. They were not publishers or priests or even professional clergymen. They lived in no vine-coated cathedral. They did not barricade themselves in a building on some Jerusalem street. They knocked on strange doors in strange communities. Why? Because the Holy Spirit gave them a deep desire to touch people for Jesus.

Now look around you. Is that a quality of people in our churches? George Webber tells about calling on all the families in a tenement building in New York. Several months afterward, a tall black man stopped him on the street with a, "Hello, Brother Webber."

Webber says, "I obviously didn't recognize the man, so he explained himself."

"You remember," he said. "You called on me a while back. I live in Building 311." (Webber had talked only half a minute through the partly closed door.) But it had made a big impresson on the man because he continued, "You know, after you left, my wife said to me, 'Reynolds, you old good-for-nothing! We've lived here in this lousy place twenty years. During that time, all kinds of people have knocked on your door. They've all come here to get you into trouble . . . to sell you drugs. That's the first time a good man has ever knocked on your door. And you didn't even let him in.' "

Webber concludes the story by saying, "Nobody had knocked on that door for Christ in twenty years. Are Christians really interested in the people in that neighborhood?"[1]

It's a fair question. Oh, we say we are. But are we? Or are we more like Charlie Brown who said: "I just love mankind. It's people I can't stand." No, sometimes when we say we are interested in people, what we really mean is that we like crowds. We are not always interested in people at all . . . not one-at-a-time. We could care less about them.

Even our obvious attempts to be concerned about people are sometimes phony. While holding a crusade in a southern Louisiana town, our team witnessed to several blacks. But when we invited them to the crusade, they told us: "Preacher, we can't come to your crusade. Blacks aren't allowed in that part of town at night." Hitch that statement to the fact that key church leaders (Sunday School teachers and deacons) also lead the Ku Klux Klan. Can you conclude that those so-called Christians are serious about touching people for the Master?

Back in medieval times, the lords had a castle with a moat around it. The moat was filled with water, and the drawbridge could be raised to keep out the unwanted. In times of war, the knights and peasants retreated into their castles. There they lived safely for weeks at a time without coming out. Then at opportune moments, they would quickly drop the drawbridge and ride out with a battalion of knights. Making a quick skirmish against the enemy, they would then dash back across the moat. And up would go the gate again.

Does that remind you of anything? Ninety-eight percent of the time, we sit in our buildings behind our moats. You would never suspect from our actions that we want anyone to get inside. In fact, you might easily assume from looking that we would rather people stay out. Then when we do come out, it is only for a quick skirmish in a revival . . . or some type of abbreviated effort that won't take up much time . . . into which we will not have to put much effort . . . and from which we can return home to rest for another eleven months and two weeks and hope that will attract people . . . after all, it is the most beautiful sanctuary in town! We write books and hope that will help people find Christ. We take out ads in the newspaper. I even heard of one church in Florida that gave out green stamps for church attendance. In short, we try to do effective witnessing by every means except the *one* that works . . . touching people personally.

Wouldn't it be strange if a doctor never saw any patients? What if a salesman never talked to any customers? Wouldn't it be unusual for a tow truck never to pull in a car . . . or a fire truck to refuse fire calls . . . or a disc jockey to sit in silence all day? But there is something stranger . . . the average apathy of Christians toward those within touching distance all around them.

In a cartoon we find Charlie Brown lying on his back on the ice. All wrapped up with fur cap, muffler, boots, and mittens, he has fallen on the ice and can't get up. The next picture shows Snoopy, the dog, coming along. He looks curiously at Charlie Brown as if to say, "What are you doing down there?" But Snoopy doesn't do anything. He just lays his head down on Charlie Brown's stomach. The last picture shows Snoopy fallen sound asleep on Charlie Brown. And Charlie concludes with, "Good grief!"[2]

We live in a world of "Snoopy Christians." We fall asleep on people's needs. We talk about them, but not to them. We can doze off and forget them, but we seldom touch anybody to help them find Christ.

In the last two decades, we concentrated on building buildings instead of loving people. We got the buildings built, but are now surprised because we didn't get the people to go in them. Maybe we need reminding that when the church had its most rapid growth . . . the years of A.D. 35 to 60 . . . it had *no church buildings.* Does this mean that we ought to eliminate all the buildings we have built and start over? Instead of burning the mortgages on the buildings, should we just burn the buildings themselves?

It probably isn't necessary to go *that far.* But it is necessary to remember that the number one duty of Christians is not to build a building. Nor is it to sing in the choir. Nor is it to serve on the church board. It isn't even to give your money. It is to reach out and touch other men for Christ.

Remember the old story of the rural insurance salesman? He was being honored at a big convention. His sales record was the highest in the company. As they gave him the award, he was asked to give his formula for success. But the poor man was scared stiff . . . more people looked up at him than he had ever seen together at one time. All he could do was mumble, "See the people . . . see the people." And perhaps that was all he needed to say.

It would be horrible to compare touching people for Christ with selling insurance. There has been too much of that! But one thing you will see if you examine a growing congregation . . . the Christians in that church have been out seeing the people. They haven't been sitting home sipping cider inside their moat.

In the third century, Simeon Stylites was very religious. He sought the highest possible spiritual development. So he built a pillar sixty feet tall. On the top of that pillar, Simeon Stylites lived for thirty years, hauling his food up on a rope. How wonderful! But how utterly worthless! While opportunities to serve Christ passed by below, he spent his total life in meditation.

Too many repeat that error. We think we are improving the organizational machine of the institution. What we are often doing is polishing our pillar (or pillow?). The rest of the time is spent in making excuses for why "nothing ever happens" in our church. We meet, we eat, we organize, we write constitutions. In our spare time, we complain about the church and its leadership. If we got down off our pillars, we might have less problems to complain about.

A sign on a bank read, "Our interest is personal." Even a bank knows that you must take a personal interest in your customers. It is time the church learned that again. It has been concerned about friendliness on Sunday morning, but that isn't enough. Our interest must be personal too.

Jesus spent little time organizing the church. He spent no time electing officers. He drew no diagrams for effective church administration. He didn't have time. He was too busy touching people. And we need to ask ourselves often, "Am I concerned about people, or am I just concerned about the local church?"

Stand back from your organizational machine. Look closely at all its moving parts. Don't measure them by how smoothly they run (the Mafia often runs smoothly too). Judge them by how much they encourage people to reach out and touch people for Jesus. Eliminate the ones that don't. How much do you have left?

Some are disturbed by the "Jesus Movement." But at least they are out to touch people. We ought to get far more concerned about that big "silent majority" that never touches anyone. They are the real enemies of the church. Peter, James, John, and Paul didn't sit around on some Jerusalem street corner whittling. Without exception, they were men up and doing . . . out touching people.

Certain Greeks came to Phillip saying, "Sir, we wish to see Jesus" (John 12:21). The masses today say the same. A vague feeling tells them he *might* be the answer to their problems. But often when they visit church, they are disappointed. They find a beautiful building and a splendid worship service, but not Jesus. Why? Because Jesus is not transmitted by organizations or buildings. He is transmitted by people who have him inside themselves.

Arnold Prater tells a story about a little boy who is afraid of the dark. Each night his mother comes into his room and tries to convince him to be unafraid. But it doesn't help. Finally, one night as he is trying to persuade her not to leave him alone, she says to him, "Son, I can't understand why you are so afraid. You're not alone. Don't you know God is with you?"

"Yes," he says, "I know that. But, Mother, I want someone with skin on!"[3]

That's the way it is with all of us. We can hear about Christ. But Christ never becomes real except through someone with skin on. And that communication begins with his being willing to get where we are . . . touch us where we live.

And when Jesus has touched us with his forgiveness, I promise, the only reason he leaves us here on earth instead of taking us on to heaven instantly is so we can be used to give "The Jesus Touch." The world looks at every Christian for peace, love, joy, happiness, purpose, meaning, and you have the answer if you know Jesus. So touch someone.

NOTES

1. George Webber, *God's Colony*, in Man's World (Nashville: Abingdon Press, 1960), p. 84.

2. Charles M. Schulz, *Here Comes Snoopy* (Greenwich, Conn: Fawcett Publications, 1966).

3. Arnold Prater, *Release from Phoniness* (Waco, Texas: Word Books, 1968), p. 83.

Chapter 11

"The Eyes of Jesus"

One reason why we're unwilling to touch people is because we don't look at them as we are supposed to . . . through the eyes of Jesus.

A hospital chaplain and a friend of mine, met a patient who was a real evangelist . . . but not for the church. He had been an alcoholic. But eight months previously he joined Alcoholics Anonymous. He monopolized the chaplain's time . . . telling him the virtues of AA . . . how much it had helped him. (Perhaps he thought a minister might easily be driven to drink and might need it someday . . . I don't know.)

Anyway, one afternoon the chaplain was drinking a cup of coffee when the cafeteria speaker system paged him. He was to go to the sixth floor to visit with his new friend. He couldn't imagine what the problem was. The man had seemed in good spirits that morning.

Arriving in the room, he found the man looking at some flowers. He asked the chaplain to read the card. It was from AA. Then he continued his praise of that group. "Now, that's what I mean. That's what makes the difference. These fellows care something about me."

During the conversation that followed, the chaplain asked him, "Why is it that you don't feel about the church like you feel about AA?"

"Simple," answered the patient. "People in the church just don't care about each other that much."

He isn't always right in that opinion. But he is right often enough to embarrass us. The wayward often find more Christian love at work, in clubs, in lodges than in the church. Some bartenders show more compassion than Christians. Not that we intend that, but it happens. How easily we imitate the elder brother in Jesus' story of the prodigal . . . the brother who shuts people out when the Father is trying to welcome them in.

Jesus had every opportunity to get negative toward people. The Pharisees were constantly on his back. The apostles could never understand what he taught them. They were jealous of each other and fought over first place in his service. They did not even understand what the kingdom of God is.

But Jesus refused to let people turn him sour. For Jesus, everybody was somebody; to him every person was a VIP. He considered a prostitute a child of God. He saw people not as they were, but as what they might become. Even at the cross, he said, "Father, forgive them; for they know not what they do" (Luke 23:34).

Jesus went out and found people. He didn't always agree with their way of life. But he did not look for their faults. He emphasized their potentials. And what miracles God could work if we would do that . . . let God's Spirit lead us to loving people instead of overlooking them.

Instead of imitating Jesus, religious people often

major in judging people. We think if we point out their sins, we will convert them. Sometimes that works; more often it fails.

Two years ago, our team was in a small Oklahoma town. One night a friend of ours from Oklahoma City brought a young man to the service with extremely long hair. He sat on the front row of the crusade audience and was very interested in being saved. After the service, many of the sainted church members showed their total disgust with his hair. They overlooked his need to know Jesus and approached him with greetings like:

"Boy, you need a hair cut."

"What are you, a boy or a girl?"

"Why don't you get your hair cut before you come back to our church?"

He was so harassed that he escaped to the rest room to get away from their criticism.

Later that night, I talked with him at length about Jesus and his need to be saved. But he was so turned off by the unloving spirits of those church members that he concluded the whole thing was fake.

Three nights later in Oklahoma City, that boy committed suicide. He was so close and yet lost for eternity because Christians became judges instead of witnesses. They failed to get down where people live and look at them through the eyes of Jesus.

A tourist driving through Michigan was interested in the great apple orchards there. Along the highway, he saw a farmer working in his trees so he stopped. The farmer was busy spraying to kill a certain kind of bug. In the conversation, the tourist said, "You must really hate those bugs!"

But the farmer replied, "Well, it is not that I am so much against bugs; it is just that I'm for apples."

And that is the key factor in witnessing. You can't just be "agin sin." That only makes you an elder brother. Yes, you should oppose unrighteousness. But, more important, you will be *for Jesus* and for him enough to believe in what he can do for even the lousiest prodigal around.

If you and I looked at more people the way Jesus did, we might be surprised at what could happen. Watch how Jesus looked at Mary Magdalene, Peter, and Matthew . . . not as they were, but for what they might become.

Standing on the eighth floor of a large hospital, I looked down across the city. It presented a shabby sight. All you could see was lots of dirty black roof tops. Later on that same day, I went downtown to run an errand. How different the view was from there. From up above you saw mostly just roof tops, but from below you could appreciate the stateliness of the buildings.

People are that way too. Look at humanity as it flows by; sometimes it looks pretty ugly. But get down among those same people. You will see much that is great and beautiful.

And if you let the Holy Spirit take charge of your life, that is where he will lead you . . . down among people. He will show you people as Jesus sees them . . . not just things walking around town but as people God loves. With that new perspective, you can accomplish things you could never do from the view up above.

Chapter 12

"When in Doubt, Read the Directions"

I've taken the last eleven chapters to say this one single thing to you . . . that witnessing comes naturally after we have been saved and filled with the Holy Spirit. We simply witness from overflow. Where did I get this gem of knowledge? . . . the Bible.

And as a witness, you are going to have to make the Bible your point of authority. Every question you face . . . ultimately God is going to be the only one who can answer.

How is true witnessing done? The answer is in the Bible. From where does the power come? The answer is in the Bible. How is a person saved? The answer is in the Bible. You see, witnessing is the battleground of Christianity, and Jesus says the Bible is our sword. Pick it up . . . read it . . . memorize it . . . devour it.

Look at the fantastic truths in it.

It is the Bible that tells us how Jesus witnessed. He met Andrew and John on a road and invited them home for dinner (John 1). He found a prostitute weeping at his feet (Luke 7). He found Zacchaeus in a tree (Luke 19). (He was an up and outer.) He witnessed to a Samaritan woman when he was thirsty at a well (John 4). Jesus even witnessed on the cross. His last living act was to win a man to himself.

The methods of the apostles are in the Bible too. They went down to the Temple and started preaching (Acts 4). When Paul entered a town, he went to the yellow pages of that day, the synagogue, and preached. That is how he won Timothy and Lydia. When they threw him out of the synagogue, he went someplace else in town (Acts 19). Aquila and Priscilla witnessed on the job; they were tentmakers. And notice that they did not argue. They did little debating. There was little of the intellectual debunking so common in our day. They simply witnessed to what had happened to them.

The Bible also tells us what our message is. Most of us know that the word "gospel" means "good news." But most Christians have no idea what the gospel really is . . . no wonder we balk at witnessing.

A prominent matron invited her doctor to dinner. She requested R.S.V.P. The doctor was prompt in his reply, but the lady couldn't make out his handwriting. Was he or was he not coming to dinner? Her husband came to the rescue. He took the note to a local druggist who had years of experience with the doctor's writing. The druggist read the scrawl, bent down, put a bottle of medicine on the counter, and said, "That will be three dollars and eighty cents please." That sounds like us and our good news. We know we have it, but we can't quite agree on what it says.

But in spite of all the confusion, there is still a simple gospel. If you look in the Bible, you can find it. Paul tells us plainly, "For I delivered to you as of first importance what I also received, that Christ died for our sins in accordance with the scriptures" (1 Cor. 15:3). And God has chosen by the preaching of this gospel . . . regardless of how foolish it may seem . . . to release, unbind, and set free all those who believe.

So when you witness, don't tell the person how wonderful your denomination is. Don't tell him about your great church, your great pastor, your great evangelist, or *your* great anything. Tell him the gospel (the good news) that Christ died and was resurrected . . . that he will save anyone who commits all to him. Then give Christ the opportunity to do just that.

A few years ago I lost my Bible. I looked in the bookshelf; I looked in the car; I looked in the desk; I looked in the reading stand, but I couldn't find it. Several months later I finally came across it. I had left it at the church. That is a symbol of what happens to a whole generation of Christians. We lose our Bibles while we are busy about church work.

This also happened to the Jews in the time of Josiah. Workmen were busy remodeling the Temple. In a back room covered with dust and rubbish, they found an ancient book. A workman gave the scroll to the priest. He gave it to the king's secretary, who discovered that it was a copy of the earliest Jewish Scriptures. No one had seen it for generations. It had been placed in the Temple for safekeeping. But because it was left there, it was lost there.

It wasn't that the Jews weren't religious, they were. Religion flourished. Along with other signs of economic prosperity, a beautiful Temple was constructed. But somehow, in the midst of all this religion, the Hebrews lost their Book. And 621 B.C.

was not the last time the Bible was lost in the church. Look at the Dark Ages in Europe. It wasn't that they had no Bibles, they did. But the only place they had them was in the churches and monasteries. It wasn't that people weren't religious, they were. But somehow, in the midst of all their religious activity, the message of the Bible got lost.

It happened again during John Wesley's time in England. Biblical study and knowledge degenerated. Many of the pastors couldn't even understand it.

Everyone talks about renewal in the church these days. Everyone seems to want it. Why then can't we get it? One reason is because we have replayed history again. We have lost the message of our Book. Where did we lose it? Someplace . . . in the church. And we won't get renewed until we find it and dust it off.

Look at the past twenty centuries. Every time the church has grown dynamic again, it was at a time when it found its Book again. In the Protestant Reformation, people began to get a copy of the Bible into their homes; they began to study it; they began to think about it; their preachers began to preach it; and the church was renewed.

It happened again in Wesley's day. The modern Methodist Church came out of a small group of English Christians who began to study the Bible together.

And the same thing is beginning to occur in our day. People are getting together in small groups for Bible study. Once again, they are trying to figure out what it means for their lives. That is a great sign. It means we are on the frontier of revival.

"But why do we keep having to study the Bible over and over?" some people ask. Any educational psychologist can answer that. Years ago a study at Northwestern University in Chicago showed that 25 percent of average people forget what they hear within one day. Another 50 percent forget what they learn within two days. Eighty-five percent forget something in four days. And 97 percent will forget something in seven days.

These are discouraging statistics for a writer. They mean that one fourth of those whose eyes pass over these lines will forget them by tomorrow. But these figures also give us the scientific reason why we must read the Bible continually . . . we forget so easily . . . much more easily than we think.

Now you may say: "But I don't really enjoy reading the Bible. I don't seem to get much out of it." That is another symptom of the central problem. The Bible is a book by, and for, the Holy Spirit to use in your life. If you are not a Christian, or if you're not letting the Holy Spirit really have his control of your life as a Christian, the Bible will be as exciting as a calculus textbook. But if you come to the Bible with the Holy Spirit leading your study, it will be a fantastic spiritual feast.

Four factors are basic to genuine Bible study. Because the Bible is so important to witnessing, I want to share them with you.

First, Bible reading must be regular.

I was in the law library at a county courthouse one day. While I waited, I pulled a law book off the shelf and began to read it. I soon gave up. I couldn't make any sense out of it. Why? I had never studied a law book before.

I was in the parts department of an automobile agency the other day. While the parts man was in the back, I thumbed through a parts book. It didn't make much sense, so I gave up. Why? I had never studied a parts book before.

I thumbed through an income tax manual at a drugstore. I decided not to buy it. I have never studied tax books, and it seemed pretty vague to me.

Studying the Bible is like that. If you don't read it on a regular basis, it will never mean anything to you. This doesn't mean you should try to read the whole thing in a week. You cannot get acquainted with your wife in a week or a month. It takes years to understand a wife, and still some days you are not quite sure. And the Bible is the same. The more you read it and live with it, the more you understand it.

Second, let the Holy Spirit lead.

The Holy Spirit is the personality of God working in the world today to lead men to Jesus.

If you go to the Bible night by night just so you can check it off as so many Christian pushups, it will mean nothing to you. But if you pick up your Bible expecting God himself to teach you and guide you, it will come alive.

The Scripture is God's way of personally leading the advance of his spiritual army into the battle against Satan. That's why it is called a sword. How stupid it would be for a soldier to go to battle without a weapon. It is just as crazy for a Christian to try to fight spiritual warfare without the Word of God.

But when you carry your sword into battle, you'll simply be sharing not what you believe, but what God says. And that brings you victory. As the Bible says, "My Word shall not return void" (paraphrase Isa. 55:11, KJV).

Several months ago Mary Mauldin of the "Three-In-One" group was studying the Word of God when, every night for almost a week, God led her to study the old Jewish Law. She kept praying the Holy Spirit would really lead her through it and teach her what he knew she needed. After a few days' steady diet of Judaism. Mary told the rest of us what was going on in her Bible study time. She said, "I don't understand why, but God is sure teaching me a lot about the Jews."

One week later, she got the answer. In the Hamilton, Ohio, Crusade, almost every night God used her to lead Jewish teen-agers to Jesus. So get into the Word of God and let the Holy Spirit lead. There are many ways the Holy Spirit will lead in your Bible study if you ask in *faith* for him to do so:

1. Through your desire when you make your desire his desires (Ps. 37:4) as he leads you to study a specific passage.
2. Through the leadership of another person.
3. Through the direct leadership of the Lord in the opening of the Scriptures.

Dr. Hallock at First Baptist Church in Norman, Oklahoma, has for years asked God to direct him as he opens the Bible to turn to the passage God has for him that day.

Third, read the Bible with an open mind.

Let it speak to *your* life and *your* situation. Read it with the open mind you use on a newspaper. Many intelligent people read the latest trashy novel with open minds. They read the latest conclusion about air pollution with open minds. They read the latest theory of a psychiatrist with open minds. But when they read their Bibles, they shut off their brains.

Paul said to the Hebrews, "For the word of God is living and active, sharper than any two-edged sword . . . discerning the thoughts and intentions of the heart" (Heb. 4:12). That is why you should read it. It can speak to you about your life, your

100

faith, your problems. Through its pages, God will put his finger into your life.

Fourth, read the Bible with other people.

We have classes in college because very few people have the discipline to study alone. They also need the stimulation of other people's thinking. Look into the New Testament. Christians met in their homes to study the Old Testament together. And if we want God to unleash his Spirit in our lives, we need to begin doing that again. Get a close friend who is in love with Jesus and meet before school each day or at the coffee break on the job and study God's Word. You'll be amazed how quickly others will want to join you.

Many years ago in London, England, there was a widow with several children. This was long before Social Security, and her husband had left her penniless. Several months behind on the rent, she felt certain she would soon be evicted. Late one evening she heard a knock at the door. Fearing it was the landlord, she did not answer it.

The next day she saw the minister. He told her he had stopped by the night before. The local church, hearing of her need, had taken up a collection to help her. He had come to bring the rent money, but she had not opened the door.

In the same way, God tries to release his power to you through his Word. But first, you must open the Book and read the instructions. Don't be afraid . . . pick it up and join the battle!

Chapter 13
"Adjust Your Fine Tuning"

"There's only one thing that still bothers me," said a speaker at a national meeting. "How do you sustain creativity and enthusiasm in the church and witnessing? We know now how to get it . . . but how do we keep it? And why does one man have it and not another? Why does a man lose it after he has it?" And he was serious. He honestly didn't know.

I wanted to stand up and say: "It is prayer. The difference between the spiritual 'haves' and 'have-nots' is prayer." No one wants to accept that. It's too old and basic an answer. But that's the whole secret. I always get, "Yeah, we know it's prayer . . . but what else?" We wouldn't have to keep looking for the "else" if we'd ever really try prayer.

The speaker continued, "We need our national leaders to tell us what we are doing that is worthwhile."

Inside I cringed. "No," I wanted to scream. "We need to pray like the disciples. Then *God* will tell us what is worth doing!"

Do you remember what the apostles did after Jesus ascended into heaven? They walked back to Jerusalem and waited in prayer for the Holy Spirit. How differently we would probably have worked it. We would have waited for a survey to be completed or a religious census to be taken. We would have called a new preacher or waited for the fall revival. But they waited for the right thing in the right way. They waited for the *Spirit* in *prayer*.

Take a look at Jesus himself. The disciples often awakened to discover Jesus missing. When they found him, he was praying. At other times, Jesus withdrew from the crowds to renew his strength. How? In prayer. If Jesus needed that, how much more must we?

Remember the extension cord? One of the primary ways you keep that cord plugged into God's power is prayer. Someone asked E. Stanley Jones for the secret of his accomplishments in witnessing. He wrote twenty-six books and preached three times a day all across India, China, and America. This went on for forty years. Jones replied, "I have always kept up my prayer life daily, so I do not have to face life all alone."[1]

Jesus said, "Abide in me. . . . He who abides in me, and I in him, he it is that bears much fruit, for apart from me you can do nothing" (John 15:4–5). And that is the way you abide in him . . . prayer. No wonder we don't feel close to Christ sometimes. If you never talked with your wife, would you feel close to her?

A TV commercial pictures an airline pilot bragging on a product. He says, "I carry Rolaids with me religiously." What a commentary on our society! We do just about everything "religiously" these days except religion. We carry our Rolaids religiously, but we have given up praying religiously. It is no wonder that some suspect God has died. Why would he stay around if nobody speaks to him?

I was touring a large city church one day. We came to a door marked, "Chapel . . . Open." But when I turned the knob, the door was locked. You and I do the same. We lock the door on Christ by refusing to talk with him.

While I was away at a meeting, a busy spider built a web across my telephone dial. That describes prayer life for many of us. A spider could build a web across our prayer connections undisturbed.

An old Chinese proverb says, "Take one step toward God, and he will take two steps toward you." That first step is prayer. If you aren't willing to take it, how can God guide your witnessing?

In the Albuquerque airport, I overheard a waitress telling someone about her trip to Japan. After describing what she had seen, she concluded by saying: "But if you don't speak the language, it's hard. I was glad to be home." And prayer is the language by which you speak with God. If you don't speak the language, it is real hard for him to have control of your life.

"Behold, I stand at the door and knock; if any one hears my voice and opens the door, I will come in to him" (Rev. 3:20). How do you open that door? By prayer.

Only when we pray every day the three great life-transforming prayers of the Bible will we become great witnesses. First, the prayer of the sinner outside the Temple: "God, be merciful to me a sinner" (Luke 18:13). Second, the prayer of Jesus in the garden: "Not as I will, but as thou wilt" (Matt. 26:39). Third, the prayer of Isaiah in the Temple: "Here I am! Send me" (Isa. 6:8).

Then after you decide to pray, the next thing you need to keep straight is what to pray *for*.

The other day someone said to me, "I'm praying that God will give me a burden."

That's commendable, but that's also the way many people glue their witnessing to a zero. They wait around for the emotional feeling of a "burden" before they can go out and witness. We need to pray instead for God to have total control over the situation . . . what we say, what we do, and the response of the person. Don't just sit around and pray for a burden. That is like praying for a truckload of money but forgetting to ask for enough gasoline to get it home.

Look at Jesus. Did he sit around on a mountain and pray for a burden? No, we can't find one example of that. He just went around telling people how to be saved.

"For God so loved the world" (John 3:16). That was the burden of Jesus. And that should be our burden too. We don't need to pray for it; we just need to pick it up from under the pew and get on with it.

If you go out, like Jesus did, you will get the burden. So, pray for one; then go get one. Take your choice. Pick the one across the street . . . down the road . . . the person you work with . . . the person you go to school with.

Real prayer always leads to action. When Moses talked with God, he was sent to do something. When Isaiah talked with God, he was sent to do something. When Jeremiah talked with God, he was sent to do something. When Jesus talked with God in the garden, God sent him to the cross. When Paul talked with God in Antioch, God sent him to the Gentiles. When Peter talked with God on the housetop, God sent him to witness. So, if you don't get sent, it may be a sign that you really weren't praying.

As you go out, keep praying. Pray for people to be saved as you talk with them. A Roman jailer would be the last person we would think of converting. But Paul and Silas prayed. and the jailer found Christ (Acts 16).

Nothing is impossible with God. And, if we pray believing that, the results are limitless. So pray that the hold of Satan in the person's life will be broken. Pray that the person can be more receptive to the Holy Spirit. That is the only way we can combat the confusion the devil thrusts on people.

I know from personal experience that prayer can be a most boring and seemingly useless experience. From early childhood we begin to pray from rote, copying what we've heard. I know adults today whose prayers echo the same thing over and over and over. But I also know that prayer can be an exciting and exhilarating experience of the daily Christian life. I want to share with you a few secrets which have revolutionized my own prayer life.

1. Speak personally to God. Forget all the "thee's" and "thou's," and remember that God is wonderfully interested in each aspect of your life. So be honest! You're not going to embarrass or surprise him!

2. Pray with someone. Find a prayer partner at school, or on the job, or down at the office, or maybe even a neighbor. And when you pray with each other claim the promise that, "Where two or more are gathered together in my name, there am I in the midst of them." Let God lead both of your hearts so that you can agree together and claim by faith his promise of victory. What an exciting bond to know that your prayer desires are being shared by another friend.

3. Establish a prayer list. Learn to pray specifically. It's even great fun to keep a written record of when you asked the prayer and when God answered it. And a prayer list will help you establish priorities and make the most out of your prayer time.

4. Use thought and conversation prayers. Many

times our team has prayer as we travel down the road together. We don't bow our heads or close our eyes, but we talk to God in a very real and meaningful way. It's the same with thought prayers. Use those moments you have alone or even in the midst of the crowd. And as Paul said, "Pray without ceasing," asking him for knowledge about that specific situation in which you're involved in that moment.

5. Learn the power and thrill of claiming by faith. There are so many promises throughout the Scriptures that are totally and completely available to us. All we have to do is claim them. Practice thanking God in advance for the fact that you know his perfect will will be accomplished.

6. Pray alone. Isaiah says,". . . in quietness and in trust shall be your strength . . . Blessed are those who wait for him" (Isa. 30:15, 18b). Notice he didn't say, "In running around looking for the answer." He didn't say, "In depending on your own strength." He didn't say, "In sitting down and doing some logical thinking." He said, "In quietness and trust." It is time we claimed that promise and power.

Make it a two-way communication system. Allow God to speak back silently to your heart . . . to prepare you mentally and spiritually and put you in the right perspective (seeing yourself as simply a tool totally in the hands of God to operate on a dying soul.) The psalmist reminds us, "Be *still* and *know* that I am God. When you are still and God gives you through that awesome, infinite silence the knowledge and awareness of just who he really is . . . then you'll *GO* and you'll *TOUCH* in *POWER!*

NOTES

1. E. Stanley Jones, *A Song of Ascents* (Nashville: Abingdon, 1968), p. 361.

**Richard Hogue is the
leader of the SPIRENO
revivals—
spiritual revolution now.**
He is a fantastically
successful young evangelist,
reaching thousands for Jesus.

CREDITS

PHOTOGRAPHY: Douglas Brachey

COVER AND FORMAT DESIGNS: O. Dixon Waters